Women in Academia

edited by
Elga Wasserman
Arie Y. Lewin
Linda H. Bleiweis

Women in Academia
Evolving Policies Toward Equal Opportunities

PRAEGER SPECIAL STUDIES IN U.S. ECONOMIC, SOCIAL, AND POLITICAL ISSUES

Praeger Publishers   New York   London

Library of Congress Cataloging in Publication Data
Main entry under title:

Women in Academia.

    (Praeger special studies in U. S. economic, social
and political issues)
    Bibliography: p.
    Includes index.
    1. Women college teachers—Legal status, laws, etc.-
United States—Addresses, essays, lectures. 2. Sex
discrimination against women—Law and legislation—
United States—Addresses, essays, lectures. I. Wasserman,
Elga Ruth. II. Lewin, Arie Y., 1935- II. Bleiweis,
Linda H.
KF4240.A75W65   344'.73'0798   74-1734
ISBN 0-275-28866-8

PRAEGER PUBLISHERS
200 Park Avenue, New York, N.Y. 10017, U.S.A.

Published in the United States of America in 1975
by Praeger Publishers, Inc.

Second printing, 1977

Printed in the United States of America

Discussions about affirmative action, the status of women, and governmental regulation in the civil rights field, both in the press and on campus, too frequently take place in a climate characterized by ignorance, misinformation, and occasionally some obvious untruths. Universities have been slow to make public their own affirmative-action plans and to disseminate details about the federal legislation applicable to institutions of higher education. This volume was prepared because the editors believe that full disclosure of the current status of equal-opportunity legislation, and a discussion of the reasons underlying this legislation, are a prerequisite to intelligent action by university communities to achieve equal treatment of women and minorities as students, staff, faculty members, and administrators.

It is our hope that the publication of this volume will make information about existing legislation in the civil rights area readily available to all members of university communities. This volume is based on the symposium "Women in Academia: Evolving Policies Toward Equal Opportunities," which was held at the 138th annual meeting of the American Association for the Advancement of Science in Philadelphia on December 30, 1971. The purpose of the conference was to bring together women in universities, university administrators, and representatives of the executive branch of the federal government to explore ways and means to achieve equal opportunities for women in universities. Specifically, it provided a forum in which members of the academic community could become familiar with legislation prohibiting discrimination in employment, could document the history of discrimination that led to the need for federal legislation, and could discuss the implications and implementation of nondiscriminatory policies for academic institutions and particularly for academic women.

At the time the symposium was held, more than 350 complaints of discrimination against academic institutions had been filed, over 200 colleges had been investigated, and more than 40 institutions had faced delays in the awarding of contracts as a result of enforcement by the Office of Civil Rights of the Department of Health, Education and Welfare of the executive order forbidding federal contractors to discriminate in employment. Before the symposium was held, Congress had enacted the Comprehensive Health Manpower Act of 1971 and the Nurse Training Amendments Act of 1971, prohibiting discrimination on the basis of sex in the admission of students to health personnel training programs receiving federal funds. Within a year after the symposium Congress enacted additional legislation: the Equal Employment Opportunity Act of 1972, extending coverage of Title VII of the 1964 Civil Rights Act to include educational institutions; and the Higher Education Act of 1972, broadening application of the Equal Pay Act of 1963 to executive, administrative, and professional employees (including faculty) and forbidding discrimination based on sex in student admissions to graduate and professional programs.

To incorporate recent developments, the original symposium papers have been updated, a few have been omitted, and several have been added. Affirmative-action requirements apply equally to efforts on behalf of minorities and of women, at all levels of institutional hierarchies. However, because there are differences between affirmative-action implementation at the academic and nonacademic levels, and between affirmative action for women and for minorities, we have chosen to focus this volume on academic women. This limitation should not be interpreted to mean that active pursuit of affirmative action in the other areas is any less urgent.

An analysis of the material in this volume should clarify the widespread misunderstanding about preferential hiring, reverse discrimination, goals and quotas, and the alleged need to lower academic hiring standards in order to achieve equity based on sex and race. These allegations have no basis in fact, but they are effective weapons in the hands of persons wishing to undermine the purposes of civil rights legislation.

We would like to take this opportunity to express our appreciation to the contributors to this volume. In addition, we wish to thank the following participants in the original symposium: Dudley E. Herschbach, Harvard University; Curtis R. Reitz, University of Pennsylvania; Margaret L. Rumbarger, formerly of the American Association of University Professors; Edward Schatz, Carnegie-Mellon University; and Ethel Bent Walsh, commissioner, Equal Employment Opportunities Commission. Finally, we wish to thank Walter G. Berl, meeting editor of the 138th AAAS Meeting for his support and cooperation in the development of the symposium that led to this volume.

CONTENTS

LIST OF TABLES

LIST OF FIGURES

Women in Academia

Within the context of the overall struggle to achieve equal rights for women in all phases of life, intensive efforts have been directed toward extending the rights of women in higher education. To understand and evaluate ongoing efforts—affirmative action programs, legislation, court actions, feminist expectations and demands—it is important to provide a background on the status of academic women.

Discrimination against women received increasing public attention in the 1960s, and extensive research was undertaken to document the alleged bias against women in academia; the results have clearly demonstrated the existence of discrimination. The most blatant and easily documented type of discrimination against women was in the area of salary. Numerous studies of salary differentials between men and women in academia indicate that salary discrimination against women is widespread and exists across disciplines, work settings, ranks, and years of experience.

There is also overwhelming evidence that women faculty are evaluated on the basis of different criteria than males at the time of the hiring decision. Contrary to popular assumptions, women remain professionally active after they obtain the Ph.D. Over 90 percent of women who earned Ph.D's in the 1950s were employed 10 years later; 80 percent were working full-time, and most had never interrupted their careers (see Figure 6.1). Seventy percent of female Ph.D. recipients, compared with 61 percent of male Ph.D. recipients, were employed in colleges and universities.[1] One might, therefore, expect to find women represented in all disciplines and at all levels of academic institutions in at least the same proportion as they are among doctorate recipients. In fact, at the financially best-endowed American universities, only 6.6 percent of the faculty were women, and only 2.6 percent of the full professorships were held by

1

women in the 1960s, even though women have consistently earned
more than 10 percent of doctoral degrees awarded since 1920. (See
Table 1.1.)

Women are still disadvantaged compared to men in the academic
job market. Surveys have shown that from 1968 to 1972 the number
of women on college faculties increased only 0.9 percent. In 1973,
even with affirmative action, only 63 percent of women who earned a
doctorate had signed teaching contracts, compared with 73 percent
for men. (See Table 1.2.)

Since the proportion of women appointed to tenure teaching positions at academic institutions has been significantly lower than the
proportion who have earned doctorates, the proportion of men appointed has been correspondingly greater than that expected from the
number of doctoral degrees awarded. As a result some men have
been appointed and promoted who might not have obtained their present positions had they been forced to compete with the total pool of
doctorate recipients rather than with the male sector only. Men have
occupied a preferred position in the academic job market, and it is
not surprising that they are reluctant to surrender it. This may explain why efforts to eliminate inequities and to encourage hiring and
promotion without regard to sex or race are now being characterized
as "discrimination" against white males. Even if a woman is hired
to a faculty position, it is very likely that she will encounter a struggle when it comes to promotion. Simply stated, "nationwide . . .
there is statistical evidence that women don't advance at the same
rate as men, for whatever reason."[2] Most women are clustered at
the lower ranks, in nonladder research and lecturer positions, and
in the less prestigious institutions.

Less frequently documented but no less real is bias against women
in university administrative positions. As stated by Rita W. Cooley,
professor of political science at New York University: "The universities tend to think automatically in terms of men when filling a new
position. In a sense it's like racism. This discrimination exists at
an unconscious level. There is no opportunity for women in administration. We are up against a strong cultural phenomenon, mass male
chauvinism. If a woman wants to be an administrator, the field is
very narrow."[3]

The specific conditions of employment provide important variables by which the status of women in academia can be evaluated.
These include rank, department affiliation, initial appointment level,
nepotism policies, leave policies (maternity, sabbaticals, leaves of
absence), fringe benefits, and retirement systems. The awarding of
faculty honors and honorary degrees, invitations as commencement
speakers, and the composition of review panels and prize-awarding
committees further reflect the status of women in academia.

TABLE 1.1

College and University Degrees Earned by Women in the United
States, Selected Years, 1900-71
(in percent)

Degree Conferred	1900	1930	1950	1960	1965	1966	1971
Total	18.9	39.5	24.4	34.2	38.5	38.4	40.9
Bachelor's (or first professional)	19.1	39.9	23.9	35.3	40.7	40.4	43.5
Master's	19.1	40.4	29.2	31.6	32.1	33.8	40.1
Doctor's	6.0	15.4	9.7	10.5	10.8	11.6	14.3

Sources: 1968 Handbook of Women Workers (Washington, D.C.:
U.S. Department of Labor, Women's Bureau, forthcoming); 1971
data from Chronicle of Higher Education, October 23, 1973, p. 8.

The scarcity of women among tenured faculty is paralleled by
the relative absence of women from scientific advisory panels of federal agencies that award research grants to universities and to individual investigators. Women receive roughly 10 percent of the doctorates in the sciences and constitute 14 percent of the scientists
listed in American Men and Women of Science, but they make up less
than 2 percent of the membership of the advisory panels of the National Science Foundation, the National Research Council of the National Academy of Sciences, and the National Institutes of Health.[4]
These groups establish priorities in allocating research funds, in
terms of both areas of investigation and support of individual scientists. The scarcity of women on these boards inevitably affects the
status of women in the scientific community.

If there had been no discrimination in the past, and none existed
now, a truly color-blind and sex-blind policy in hiring or admissions
might be equitable; in the light of past discrimination, however,
"equal treatment" without affirmative efforts to redress past imbal-
ances would perpetuate the status quo. The Supreme Court has recognized that in the real world the scars of past discrimination have
gone too deep and that "neutral" remedies are too often ineffective.
Affirmative action, including goals and timetables, has been upheld
in court decisions. In each case there was a recognition of the fact
that equal treatment of groups discriminated against in the past is

TABLE 1.2

Employment Status of Ph.D. Recipients Within Three Months of Receipt of Degree, 1960-73

Year Earned Degree	Sex	Signed Contracts	Negotiating	Seeking/No Prospect	Other	Postdoctoral Study
1960 (N = 9,734)	Male	82	8	6	4	7
	Female	73	8	12	7	6
1965 (N = 16,341)	Male	80	8	5	7	11
	Female	72	9	10	9	10
1967 (N = 20,385)	Male	81	7	4	7	11
	Female	73	9	10	9	10
1968 (N = 22,916)	Male	80	7	5	8	11
	Female	70	9	12	9	10
1969 (N = 25,721)	Male	79	8	7	6	14
	Female	67	9	16	8	13
1970 (N = 29,436)	Male	78	8	9	5	15
	Female	65	10	17	8	13
1971 (N = 31,851)	Male	77	7	12	5.2	n.a.
	Female	65	9	19	6	n.a.
1973 (N = 33,727)	Male	73	8	14	5.2	n.a.
	Female	63	11	20	8	n.a.

Note: Postdoctoral study is figured as a percent of total, and the percentage of employment status is figured as percent of total minus the number of postdoctoral fellowship recipients.

Source: Data from National Academy of Sciences, Office of Scientific Personnel, 1974.

not enough to create equal opportunities; positive steps must be taken
by institutions to attract and include groups formerly unwelcome.

The legitimacy of engaging in affirmative action to correct past
inequities and to assure access to universities of underrepresented
groups discriminated against in the past was affirmed by Professor
Archibald Cox, in a brief submitted to the Supreme Court on behalf
of Harvard College, in support of the admissions policy of the University of Washington School of Law:

> In recent years many institutions of higher educa-
> tion have determined that their objectives should include
> removing the special obstacles facing disadvantaged mi-
> nority groups in access to higher education, business and
> professional opportunities, and professional services —
> obstacles which are deeply-ingrained consequences of
> the hostile public and private discrimination pervading
> the social structure. Giving favorable weight to minor-
> ity status in selecting qualified students for admission
> is an important method of reducing these disadvantages.
>
> Neither the pursuit of this objective nor the means
> adopted is beyond the scope of educational policy-making
> discretion under the Equal Protection Clause. The
> Equal Protection Clause does not prohibit all racially-
> conscious government activity, but only that which is
> "hostile" or "invidious" towards minorities without com-
> pelling justification; or which occurs in relation to a
> "fundamental right" without compelling justification; or
> which falls under the general constitutional ban against
> arbitrary or capricious classification. Giving an advan-
> tage in law school admissions in order to reduce the dis-
> advantages suffered by member[s] of minority groups long
> subject to pervasive discrimination, is neither "hostile"
> nor "invidious."[5]

The real motivation of individuals who attack affirmative-action
legislation surfaces only rarely. Few persons possess the candor
of Paul Seabury, professor of government at the University of California at Berkeley, who asserted at a conference, sponsored by the
International Council of the Future of the University, in New York
that the changes facing American campuses were due in part to a
shift in the public's expectations of higher education. A critic of the
federally enforced affirmative-action program, Professor Seabury
declared: "Demands that universities become agencies for social
change by extending opportunities to minority groups and women have
changed the universities from an ivory tower to a public utility."[6]

Many academicians share Professor Seabury's nostalgia for the ivory tower, but few state their opposition to affirmative action as candidly. Instead, they debate the wisdom of making university records available to the government or argue that it is impossible to establish meaningful hiring goals.

These underlying attitudes are discussed by Lilli Hornig, Lenore Weitzman, Mary Bunting, and other contributors to this volume. J. Stanley Pottinger, the chief architect of the government's affirmative-action policy pertaining to the hiring of minorities and women by academic institutions, explains what affirmative action does and does not mean in the chapter entitled "Race, Sex, and Jobs: The Drive Toward Equality." Bernice Sandler reviews the legislation pertaining to equal opportunity and nondiscrimination in academic institutions in the chapter "Sex Discrimination, Educational Institutions, and the Law: A New Issue on Campus."

The understanding of the legal requirement of affirmative action is only the first step in equalizing opportunities for women at academic institutions. Ultimately each institution must set its own goals and devise an affirmative action plan compatible with its particular academic program and administrative structure. As a model for such a plan, this volume includes the complete affirmative-action plan of Stanford University with introductory notes by Ann Miner. The drafting and implementation of effective affirmative-action programs is discussed by Lenore Weitzman. Elizabeth Scott develops a methodology for setting hiring goals and analyzing salary differentials and hiring pools in "Developing Criteria and Measures of Equal Opportunities for Women."

Two chapters in the book touch on more specific aspects of efforts to increase the participation of women in academic life and illustrate experiences on particular campuses. Ruth Beach presents a case history of affirmative action at Carnegie-Mellon University, and Alice Cook describes her experiences as the first ombudsman at Cornell University.

The struggle for equal opportunities for academic women in the years ahead will be a difficult one even with the wholehearted support of administrators and faculty--a goal not yet achieved. Real progress can be measured only by an increased ratio of women to men in the tenured ranks. Since budgetary constraints are forcing cutbacks in faculty size at most institutions, few new tenure appointments can be expected in the years ahead; and opportunities for appointing women will, therefore, remain limited. It is thus critical that appointments to nontenured ranks go to outstanding women and minority candidates, so that these candidates can compete successfully for the small number of tenure slots that will become available. It is important to avoid the temptation to respond to pressures for af-

firmative action by recruiting and appointing individuals who are unlikely to become serious contenders for later promotions. This practice represents "sexist" or "racist" hiring at its worst and is not ap-
parent from statistical progress reports. It can be detected only by
comparing the turnover rates over time between men and women, department by department, for each university.

The success or failure of affirmative-action programs will ultimately depend on the commitment, energy, and courage of those faculty members and administrators in a position to influence recruiting, hiring, and admissions policies, and on the active interest and
support of other campus groups. Continued vigilance and efforts are
essential if paper plans are to have any lasting effects. Affirmative-
action efforts on behalf of women and minorities must be coordinated.
If disadvantaged groups allow themselves to become divided and to
compete with each other, affirmative action for all groups will be
slowed. If students and nontenured women have to shoulder the primary burden of demanding implementation of affirmative-action plans,
their careers will suffer. Those women who have "made it" must
give their support and encouragement to younger women whose repu-
tations are not yet securely established. Finally, dedication and commitment to affirmative action efforts by individuals is often informal
and necessarily sporadic. To be effective, affirmative action must
be institutionalized by devising formal procedures that assure participation by the central administration in departmental recruiting, appointment, and tenure decisions.

NOTES

1. H. Astin, The Woman Doctorate in America (New York: Russell Sage Foundation, 1969), p. 72.

2. Wall Street Journal, June 30, 1971, p. 1.

3. A. S. Harris, "The Second Sex in Academe," AAUP Bulletin
56 (September 1970).

4. J. Apter, "Increasing the Professional Visibility of Women
in Academia: A Case Study," in W. T. Furniss and P. A. Graham,
eds., Women in Education (Washington, D.C.: American Council
on Education, 1974), p. 104.

5. DeFunis vs. Odegard, 416U.S.312, 1974.

6. New York Times, March 19, 1974, p. 22.

AFFIRMATIVE ACTION
THROUGH AFFIRMATIVE
ATTITUDES
Lilli S. Hornig

Affirmative action in universities, bringing with it the necessity for locating, recruiting, hiring, and promoting women, seems to produce even more malaise among academic administrators than discussions of budgets. Unpleasant as the topic of finances may be, it is at least something with which they feel familiar. But women as something other than secretaries, wives, or sex objects—women as serious students, professional colleagues, or even authority figures —are a whole new dimension in academic life. While everyone seems to subscribe in principle to the idea of full professional equality for women, implementing that principle is a difficult and often acrimonious process.

The enhancement of antipathy between the sexes often seems to be the outcome of affirmative-action discussions. Women become more bitter as they review the results of past discrimination and contemplate the slow pace of improvement, and men become more aggressive as they are made to feel guilty about a situation for which most of them bear little blame individually. Nonetheless, the law now requires us all either to act out that natural antipathy in a new context or to accommodate ourselves peacefully to the new necessities. In this chapter I would like to explore some of the important problems involved in the process of accommodation.

LINGERING STEREOTYPES

I think it is well to remember that all of us, male and female, are the products of the Freudian age in academia. Freud was surely not the first man to bolster his own already considerable ego by putting down women, but he _was_ probably the first man since St. Paul whose ideas on the subject became so institutionalized. Briefly, he believed that women are anatomically deprived and therefore also psychologically incomplete and inferior, useful chiefly as bearers of children and comforters of men. From this he developed the theory, further elaborated by modern psychologists all the way to Erik Erikson, that men are by nature aggressive, enterprising, resourceful, and active, while women are submissive, docile, accommodating, and passive—all more or less pejorative terms. Moreover, any woman who cannot or will not fit herself into this stereotype and resign herself to a second-class role in life is by definition a defective specimen. Right up until the present, psychologists have wondered why women have so much trouble adjusting to their "proper" role that three times as many women as men require psychiatric counseling or treatment.

Myths about what women can and cannot do pervade our lives, in and out of the university. Women get good grades but have no imagination. They do well in humanities but not in science. They are good at routine work but do not have ideas. They may have jobs, but they should not have careers. They work for pin money, to buy luxuries, not to support themselves or anyone else. You may entrust your children's lives to them, but they have no sense of responsibility. When they get a notion, they'll nag you to death; but they have no perseverance and drive. You may let them drive the children to school and your aged mother to the hospital, but you can't wait to tell the latest "woman driver" joke. Family cooking has to be done by women, but chefs are men. The list can be extended almost indefinitely.

In the academic context, each of us will have to recognize these ingrained discriminatory attitudes within ourselves before we can make much progress toward overcoming them. The concept of affirmative action is a tool designed to facilitate the equalization of opportunities for employment; as such it bypasses the underlying problem of attitudes, but presupposes that everyone truly desires a world of equal opportunity for men and women of all races and creeds. Unfortunately this assumption is not yet justified; affirmative-action programs are so bitterly criticized precisely because when equal opportunity is granted to all, those who have heretofore been privileged will have to give up some of what they regard as their natural prerogatives.

To me this is not a matter for negotiation around a conference table. I do not intend to bargain with anyone for the basic human rights that the law and (soon, I hope) the Constitution guarantee to me. But I do intend to see that those guarantees are enforced, by whatever means necessary.

Martha Peterson has recently pointed out that the application of civil rights legislation to educational institutions merely requires these institutions to translate into action the moral principles of equality that they have long espoused in theory.[1] If the universities had themselves willingly undertaken the responsibility for living as they professed to teach others to do, they would not now be facing the specter of government intervention in their internal affairs. While one may rightly question whether universities are suitable institutions for spearheading social change, they do unquestionably bear the responsibility for making certain that basic human rights are safeguarded within their own establishments.

PRESENT STATUS OF WOMEN IN ACADEMIA

Even a quick survey of the present status of women in academia makes it plain that the universities have not discharged that responsibility. There is discrimination at all levels. College admissions practices are blatantly discriminatory toward women in major ways. Fewer women than men are admitted—the national ratio now stands at 46 percent women and 54 percent men; while the ablest girls can all get into some college, the best and most selective universities maintain an average ratio of only 40:60,[2] which means that many of our best women cannot get the best education offered. The highly selective private universities have even lower proportions of women. Women of average ability stand a much lower chance of being admitted at all than men in that category. Some colleges even make sure that traditional stereotypes are not disturbed by selecting their applicants to fit expectations; one institution, for example, admits equal percentages of male and female candidates with verbal SAT scores over 700, but admits 91 percent of males and only 85 percent of females with mathematical SAT scores in the highest range.[3] Thus the conventional belief in the mathematical superiority of men is neatly substantiated.

As one moves from college admissions to tenure level and top administration, women become progressively scarcer; but it is interesting to note that the two biggest drops occur between the master's and doctoral degrees and between nontenured and tenured ranks. More women than men drop out of graduate school without completing doctorates; much of this may indeed be due to societal pressures, role modeling, and family responsibilities. But when one considers the active discrimination against women in graduate schools (documented, for instance, in the Berkeley report),[4] and when one takes into account the lower earning capacity and bleak academic employment prospects, the surprising thing is not how few women complete their doctorates, but how many do. It is interesting to note, too, that their share of doctorates, nationwide and across all disciplines, has risen from about 10 percent to a little over 13 percent in the last decade.[5]

That there is indeed plenty of discouragement cannot be doubted, and much of it comes at the critical juncture between junior and senior faculty appointments. Until the recent job shortage it had not been unduly hard for women to obtain short-term appointments as instructors and even assistant professors; and they were always welcome in such off-ladder posts as lecturers. The universities needed teachers for the ever-growing student bodies, and women were moderately acceptable as teachers. So they were hired, in proportions roughly comparable with their presence in the doctorate population, for these lower, nontenured ranks. They were paid less than men with equivalent qualifications and given different and less prestigious responsibilities—heavier teaching loads and therefore less time for research; less research support and more student counseling; less service on prestige committees and more on the invisible but time-consuming ones. Women faculty members are found predominantly in two- and four-year colleges and in women's colleges, as opposed to universities, and are, therefore, even less likely to achieve visibility and professional recognition. They are concentrated heavily in the lowest ranks: of all the women on faculties, almost 35 percent are instructors and another 29 percent are assistant professors; only about 9 percent of them achieve full professorships nationally, the majority in home economics, languages, and education. At prestige universities at most 2 to 3 percent of full professorships are held by women. There is another quantum jump at the top administrative level, where only 0.7 percent of presidents are lay women; and their numbers still declining.

The end result of the process is summarized by the figures on academic salaries gathered by the American Council on Education.[6] Almost two-thirds of all the women employed on college and university faculties earn less than $10,000 a year, while only about 28 percent of the men are in this lowest category. But the picture changes rapidly as we go up the salary scale. The percentage of men in the $14,000 to $20,000 range is three times as large as the percentage of women, and over $20,000 it is 5.5 times as large. The actual numbers of men employed in all ranks are, of course, much greater than the numbers of women, by about 500 percent.

GOALS AND QUOTAS

I mention these unpalatable facts not just for the purpose of doing a little sly consciousness-raising, but because they form the neces-

sary background to a discussion of affirmative attitudes. In order to
decide where we need to go and how we can get there, we need first
to know where we are and how we got there.

Effective affirmative action has two distinct aspects: nondiscrimination in all hiring, promotion, and other employment practices;
and the establishment of goals and timetables directed toward achieving a truly nondiscriminatory situation. It is the second of these efforts that is causing the most bitter controversy because it is so easy
to attack on unrelated grounds; it is questioned, for example, on the
ground that goals are hard to distinguish from quotas — and we all
know too well how quotas may be used to exclude rather than include.

Nonetheless, I do not find it too difficult to make the semantic
and conceptual distinction between a quota, which traditionally operates as a ceiling on numbers, and a goal, which is an end to which one
aspires and which one hopes to reach. The establishment of goals
and timetables is also attacked because it is thought to expose universities to undue outside interference. Goals and timetables involve
evaluation, disclosure of certain records, and government meddling
in institutional affairs. Affirmative action does entail certain very
limited problems in the areas of institutional autonomy and academic
freedom, but to argue that a law is inapplicable because it does not
conform to established practice is not valid.

I do not want to debate the implementation of guidelines in detail,
but to focus instead on the principle of nondiscrimination in academic
employment practices. It is never openly challenged because it
would be unacceptable to do so, yet it is in this area that some of the
most fundamental problems arise. The argument most widely advanced in support of the status quo, and thus in nonsupport of nondiscrimination, is the argument of quality. Faculties and administrations in whose ranks women and minority group members are grossly
underrepresented or totally absent will maintain staunchly that they
hire only the most qualified person, who almost always turns out to
be a white male. The litany of reasons for not hiring a woman candidate, provided one appears on the list at all, is extensive. If she is
unmarried, that is ground for suspicion — what's wrong with her?
If she decides to get married, she'll certainly leave. If she is married, what if she should have children? If she already has children —
well, she can't be seriously interested in an academic job; she ought
to be home taking care of them; she'll never be available when you
need her. If she is divorced, she's obviously unstable and untrust-
worthy. All these statements can be documented. You will note that
none of these reasons has the remotest connection with academic
quality, yet they are frequently cited. It should be pointed out that
if they are given as justification for not hiring a particular woman,
they are all actionable in court.

A second common body of reasons does deal with qualifications, though not necessarily with quality. It contains such statements as, for example, that women only want to teach, not do research, and a quality faculty must do both. Whether the statement is true is hard to ascertain. Women on faculties do comparatively more teaching and less research, but it is not possible to establish that they do so from choice and not necessity. Female department members tend to be hired for the "teaching" jobs and are seldom encouraged in their research or rewarded for it with grants, prizes, and other honors. On the other hand, the ranks of research personnel, as opposed to straight faculty positions, are filled with women—all doing research. This happens, of course, because such positions are less prestigious, not on the tenure ladder, and therefore more accessible to women. The situation is rather like that in other areas where discrimination exists. In industry, for example, women are routinely found in dull, repetitive jobs, such as assembling small components, because it is said that they excel at fine work; that the work is grossly underpaid is not mentioned. In medicine, on the other hand, where surgery is the most lucrative specialty, men must plainly be much better at fine work, because almost all surgeons are men.

Another frequently cited reason for not promoting women is that although their routine academic ability seems to be excellent, they somehow lack the drive and motivation required for the top positions. Like so many of the arguments in the whole field, this is another self-fulfilling prophecy. Women quite obviously need more drive and motivation than men to persist at all in academic pursuits, and a woman who has achieved even an assistant professorship is in all likelihood both better qualified and more highly motivated than her male colleagues. If discriminatory practices block her route to advancement, no amount of drive will get her there.

The assumption underlying all these arguments is that in order to hire more women for faculty positions, standards will have to be lowered. Implicit in that assumption is the thesis that in this best of all possible academic worlds, recruiting and selection processes have always operated to produce, by definition, the best of all possible faculty members. It takes only a cursory look at any faculty in the country to demonstrate that this is not true. The usual limited recruiting procedures for academic posts, best described as the old-boy network, have in effect operated to exclude women and minorities, and have created academic departments self-selected to perpetuate their established images. This practice is not only discriminatory but also accounts in large measure for the rigidity of academic tradition that fueled so much of the disruption of the 1960s.

The fact is, of course, that any new faculty appointment entails a certain risk; and not all appointees can be expected to pan out. A young candidate of limited experience and background must be evaluated in terms of future promise and ultimate potential for sound teaching and brilliant scholarship, with the hope that these qualities will eventually reflect credit on the institution. This risk is peculiar to the nature of the academic enterprise. For example, while hiring for a corporation also entails the problem of estimating potential on the basis of very limited past history, there are more possibilities for burying the recruiter's mistakes. The person hired can, for instance, be moved horizontally to a more suitable job, such as from research into marketing. In an academic hierarchy this is not possible; and if you are not good enough to move up, you have to move out. During a period of rapid expansion like the 1960s, of course, there was more opportunity for people of less than top talent to move up than there is now or will be in the foreseeable future.

What makes these considerations relevant to affirmative action as it applies to women is that if you read a great many resumes and dossiers, as I do, a curious fact emerges: A young man is routinely evaluated in terms of his future promise, because that is what everyone is used to doing. But a young woman is not really believed to have a future and is almost invariably evaluated only in terms of past performance. In practice, this means that a woman must, for instance, have had practical experience in administration before she can become even a middle-level administrator. A man, on the other hand, may leapfrog the intermediate stages, as President Goheen did at Princeton when he was promoted to the presidency directly from an assistant professorship in classics. Indeed, as Dean Jacquelyn Mattfeld's study shows, most top administrators of prestigious colleges or universities come directly from the senior faculty without previous administrative experience, other than perhaps a department chairmanship.[7] Simply because so few women, and those quite clearly exceptional ones, have attained prominent positions in the past, it is now difficult for people to project the same criteria of future success for young women that they routinely apply to young men. I believe it is largely for this reason that the various irrelevant arguments relating to marital status, motherhood, and housewifely duties are so often cited. At any rate, those traditional female factors constitute the only frame of reference within which most people are used to evaluating women. While such considerations are in fact relevant to a discussion of acceptable working conditions for women, an aspect to which I will return shortly, they have nothing to do with quality.

As a first step, then, we will have to discard some of the myths and legends surrounding academic women and have a look at the facts

instead. Perhaps the most persistent and insidious myth is that while
women have been given expensive training, and many actually have
doctorates, they really are not fully committed to their profession.
They work part-time, it is said, because they somehow do not care
enough to work full-time. This is easy to test by offering good full-
time positions along with day care and reasonable maternity leave policies, the latter now mandatory. In any case it is not readily demonstrable that the quality of scholarly output is related to time spent;
and even the quantity of work done does not show a simple dependence
on full-time status, as will be evident if you examine the publication
record of any average department. Another legend says women, especially married women with children, are not interested in scholarship
and do not publish. This is not supportable by facts either.

Another popular myth is that women are professional dropouts,
and that even if they do complete a Ph.D., M.D., or law degree,
they will not practice a profession for any length of time. Thus scarce
fellowship funds and academic posts are wasted on women who will
not stay in the profession long enough to do credit to it. The facts
are very different. Helen Astin's studies of academic women demonstrate that there is a direct relationship between the amount of education a woman has had and the length of time she stays in her profession. They show, further, that 91 percent of women who hold doctorates are still practicing their professions full-time 10 years after receiving the degree, despite marriage; and 81 percent of women doctorate-holders with children are employed full-time.[8] As almost any
professor with some experience can testify, not nearly all male doctorate-holders practice the professions for which they underwent long
and costly training, usually at public expense. In the case of men,
however, such professional mobility is counted an asset; the doctoral
or law degree confers added prestige on many a corporate or government official. Although it contributes very little directly to his professional capacity, no one would argue that his academic training was
wasted because he eventually turned to a different field.

For women the situation is quite different; training and experience
are assumed to qualify them only for the narrow areas for which they
prepared specifically. It is another aspect of our inability to see women's potential for future success in the male frame of reference.
We have gradually learned to expect that if a woman has demonstrated
success as a teacher or even as a scholar, she may continue that
career successfully. But we cannot envision, as we do all the time
for men, that if she brings originality and creative flair to her teaching or scholarship, she may be capable of applying those same qualities to other activities: top administration, a department chairmanship, a government consultancy, or membership on a board of directors. I believe it is this problem, which President Mary Bunting of

Radcliffe termed the "climate of nonexpectation," that persistently keeps women on the wrong side of the tenure barrier and thus at the bottom of the ladder to academic success.

One of the most articulate and widely heard critics of affirmative action has been John Bunzel, president of California State University at San Jose. While paying due deference to the principle of nondiscrimination, he attacks the efforts to redress the balance by implementing affirmative-action programs as "reverse discrimination" based on the introduction of false criteria such as race and sex; and he strongly defends the traditional academic recruiting, hiring, and promotion practices as being based on individual merit rather than consideration of such class attributes. We might inquire, first of all, why he labels discrimination "reverse" when applied to white males. There seems to be a tacit assumption here that white males should be preferred, and that anything else is contrary to the natural order of things. Second, we have seen that the "false" criteria of race and sex have indeed been with us for a long time, and I could not agree more strongly that they have no place in a university. None of us would wish to make a case for hiring, preferentially or otherwise, women or minority group members who are truly not qualified. We are just as concerned as men with the maintenance of academic quality —and for the same reasons, because we prefer to be associated with good institutions rather than mediocre ones and because we believe in excellence for its own sake and wish to preserve it. We simply do not believe that excellence is associated only with white males.

Neither do we believe that the requirements for more open and broadly based recruiting efforts are in any way infringements of academic freedom and institutional autonomy. The right of universities to be free of the control of the state extends to the areas of intellectual inquiry, the subject matter of teaching, and the policies that serve those purposes, but not to the treatment of individuals by the institution. The university's existence within the larger framework of society is already governed by the laws of that society, and is dependent on financial and moral support from that society. Thus its autonomy is circumscribed by a great many constraints and considerations—what programs taxpayers, legislatures, or alumni will or will not support, and in some deplorable cases even which faculty members may or may not be hired because of public opinion. But the autonomy of the university does not supersede the laws that safeguard the rights of individuals. Affirmative-action guidelines do not dictate that a woman or a black must be hired in preference to a white male regardless of qualifications, however often or loudly their opponents choose to interpret them that way. They do dictate, however, that irrelevant considerations of race and sex may not be used to abridge an in-

dividual's right to a fair assessment of her or his qualifications for a
position—no more and no less. If universities consider that mandate
an infringement of their institutional autonomy, they lay themselves
open to the question of whether they deserve to be autonomous at all.

Academic freedom, on the other hand, is the right of the individual to study and teach what her or his mind dictates, not what the
state or the institution prescribes. Like all kinds of freedom, it is
not absolute and it is fragile. It is subject to erosion by many influences and pressures—by the same financial, moral, and legal limitations that define institutional autonomy and by considerations of personal advancement and even profit; but not by nondiscriminatory personnel practices.

IMPLICATIONS OF AFFIRMATIVE ACTION

Underneath all of the rhetoric against affirmative action and the
roadblocks being put in the way of its implementation there runs a
current of fear that the growing presence of women on the campus
will produce a change in the nature of the academic enterprise. Of
course it will. We are a long way from perfection in our universities,
and any change that will broaden the base of intellectual inquiry and
lay the foundations of more truly human social practices can only be
for the better.

As a scientist I know that men and women are different in many
ways, both obvious and subtle, and undoubtedly in some ways we do
not know about yet. Possibly they differ intellectually. All the measures established so far, mostly by men, do not show that; but I
cannot rule out the possibility that more careful research, perhaps
by women, would. At any rate, it seems certain that there are no
significant differences in intellectual capacity, though there may well
be differences in intellectual orientation. We are not likely to know
until universities stop trying to assess women by how far we deviate
from the male norm and society stops trying to force us all into the
Freudian female stereotype.

As a first step we need working conditions in the universities
that take account of the obvious differences between men and women.
There is no reason why maternity leave cannot be granted on the same
basis as any other medical leave, with appropriate benefits and full
retention of seniority. Child-rearing leaves, for students or faculty,
are no more disruptive than leaves for military or other government
service. Part-time appointments with full professional status can
make more diverse talents available at almost no increase in cost,
and can broaden an institution's outlook by rooting it more solidly in
daily human concerns. They would probably benefit the institution

even more than the individual. A more liberal view of part-time
study, especially at the graduate level, along with loosening of the
lockstep approach to credit and degree requirements, would open up
a new talent pool.

What if there were more fundamental changes? What if it turns
out that women really have different intellectual interests? That they
are more concerned with keeping the earth liveable than with coloniz-
ing the moon? That they would rather work on better transportation
systems or better medical care than on a better military rocket?
Would it be so destructive of the male ego to learn more about what
it is to be human—for both males and females? Isn't half the human
race worthy of more honest intellectual inquiry? Might it not be that
we would all redirect our efforts toward the greater benefit of human-
ity instead of its destruction? Are the worlds that men have made
and the universities that they have constructed to suit their requirements really so perfect that there is no room for improvement?

Some time ago Edgar Berman, a prominent physician, thundered
that the "raging storms of female hormones" affect women's judgment,
rendering them unfit to assume serious responsibilities and make decisions. "What," he asked desperately, "would have happened if a
woman had been in charge at the Bay of Pigs?" He got his answer
from Estelle Ramey, herself an endocrinologist and president-elect
of American Women in Science: "Well, fellow, what did happen at
the Bay of Pigs?"

In many ways we women find ourselves in a Bay of Pigs situation.
From our point of view, things could hardly be much worse; and support of the purposes of affirmative action is surely an essential step
in eliminating persisting discrimination. The hardest problem we
face is that of deeply ingrained attitudes and sexual stereotypes, and
it is time to try some new approaches. Even the most basic problems
can yield to novel solutions.

NOTES

1. Martha E. Peterson, "Keynote Address, 55th Annual Meeting
of American Council on Education, 1972," in W. T. Furniss and P.
A. Graham, eds., Women in Higher Education (Washington, D.C.:
American Council on Education, 1974), pp. 7-9.

2. The American Freshman: National Norms for Fall 1971
(Washington, D.C.: Office of Research, American Council on Education, 1971), p. 16.

3. K. Patricia Cross, "The Woman Student," "Background Papers for Participants in the 55th Annual Meeting of the American
Council on Education, 1972," in Furniss and Graham, op. cit., p. 34.

4. University of California at Berkeley, "Report of the Subcommittee on the Status of Academic Women on the Berkeley Campus" (Berkeley, the Academic Senate, May 19, 1970).

5. Earned Degrees Conferred, Annual Reports, U.S. Office of Education, U.S. Government Printing Office, 1960-74.

6. Juanita M. Kreps, "Background Papers for Participants in the 55th Annual Meeting of the American Council on Education, 1972," in Furniss and Graham, op. cit., p. 61.

7. Jacquelyn A. Mattfeld, "Many Are Called, but Few Are Chosen," in Furniss and Graham, op. cit., pp. 121-27.

8. H. S. Astin, The Woman Doctorate in America (New York: Russell Sage Foundation, 1969), p. 57.

3

SEX DISCRIMINATION, EDUCATIONAL INSTITUTIONS, AND THE LAW: A NEW ISSUE ON CAMPUS

Bernice Sandler

One of the most remarkable, but little noted, achievements of the 92nd Congress during 1971-72 was the shaping of a new national policy to end sex discrimination in all educational institutions at all levels, including students, staff, and faculty, from nursery school to postgraduate education.

The speed with which the Congress extended Title VII of the Civil Rights Act of 1964 to include all educational institutions—amending the Equal Pay Act of 1963 to cover executive, administrative, and professional employment; amending the Public Health Service Act to cover admissions to all health profession training programs; enacting Title IX of the Education Amendments Act of 1972 to cover all phases of student treatment, including admissions; and added sex discrimination to the jurisdiction of the U.S. Commission on Civil Rights[1]—indicates that it was acutely aware of discrimination against women in our educational institutions. There was virtually no opposition to the passage of these laws by either the educational community or the public at large. Sex discrimination, once only a philosophical or moral issue, is now a legal issue as well. These laws are not merely employment laws; they are civil rights laws with a different legislative and judicial history.

Academics have been puzzled and somewhat bewildered by the impact of these new laws. Many institutions holding federal contracts

---

Reprinted by permission from Journal of Law & Education 2, no. 4 (1973): 613-35. The Journal is published quarterly by Jefferson Law Book Company, 646 Main Street, Cincinnati, Ohio 45201. Journal of Law & Education, 728 National Press Building, Washington, D.C. 20004.

had already felt the sting of the federal government under Executive Order 11246 as amended, which requires all federal contractors to end discrimination in employment and to have a written plan of affirmative action. This order, coupled with the new legislation, has raised new questions and concerns as the academic community seeks to understand the implications of federal law and regulations.

EXECUTIVE ORDER 11246 AS AMENDED
BY EXECUTIVE ORDER 11375

The executive order covers only institutions that hold federal contracts. It prohibits discrimination in employment, and does not cover students, except insofar as they are employed by the institution. The executive order is not law, but a series of rules and regulations that contractors agree to follow when they accept a federal contract. Its main provision is that the contractor must have a written plan of affirmative action* to "remedy the effects of past discrimination" and to prevent the continuation of current discrimination. It is not enough to agree to cease discriminating. Employers who do not have a written plan (or who fail to follow it) may lose their federal contracts. The Department of Labor, through its Office of Federal Contract Compliance, is responsible for all policy matters under the executive order; the Department of Health, Education and Welfare, however, does the actual review and enforcement at universities and colleges.

Revised order no. 4 details the requirements for affirmative action plans. As a minimum, institutions must do the following:

1. Develop a data base on all job classifications
2. Have a policy statement forbidding discrimination
3. Appoint an individual to be in charge of the program
4. Examine recruiting, hiring, promotion policies, salaries, and all other conditions of employment.
5. Identify areas of underutilization and develop specific plans to overcome these areas
6. Develop numerical goals and timetables.

Affirmative action and the issue of numerical goals are controversial. Affirmative action is not only required of federal contractors; it can

---

*Contractors with $50,000 worth of contracts and 50 employees must have a written affirmative action plan. Public institutions were previously exempted from the requirement of having a written plan; in January 1973, that exemption was deleted.

also be required under Title VII of the Civil Rights Act of 1964 if a finding of discrimination has been made. The U.S. Commission on Civil Rights has defined affirmative action to be "steps taken to remedy the grossly disparate staffing and recruitment patterns that are the present consequence of past discrimination and to prevent the occurrence of employment discrimination in the future."[2]

A plan must be based on an analysis of all conditions of employment: policies and practices affecting (but not limited to) recruiting, hiring, job classification, salaries, fringe benefits, promotion, terminations. All job classifications for all employees must be analyzed in terms of race, sex, and ethnicity for each organizational unit and pay grade. Where underutilization occurs, numerical goals must be developed.

Numerical goals are often confused with quotas; the terms are often erroneously used interchangeably. However, the government and the courts have made a clear distinction between the two: goals are legal; quotas clearly violate the Constitution and numerous federal statutes. Quota systems keep people out; goals are targets for inclusion of people previously excluded. Goals are an attempt to estimate what the employer's work force would look like if no illegal discrimination based on race or sex had ever existed. The institution develops the goals when "underutilization" occurs; and they are aligned with the number or percentage of qualified women and minorities available, not in terms of general representation in the population. If an employer fails to meet the goals, he then has to show that he made a good-faith effort to recruit, hire, and promote women, and must produce records documenting those efforts.* For example, the department chairperson may show that he or she has contacted women's groups (such as the women's caucuses relevant to the discipline), has called individual women scholars for referral of candidates, has included in letters to colleagues and in job advertisements statements like "women and minorities, including minority women, are welcome to apply," and has also evaluated the women already in the department who might qualify for the opening. If, after all this, it turns out that all the women who were considered were poorly qualified and the man hired was indeed the best-qualified applicant, the employer can document a good-faith effort at affirmative action and thus can justify his decision to hire the white male. If this is the case, the employer has discharged his obligation under the executive order; the obligation to meet the goal is not absolute.

There is no requirement whatsoever that would force academicians to hire less-qualified women or minorities; if the best-qualified

---

*In most instances the academic employer is a "he."

person is white and male, then that person can be hired. * What the employer must be able to demonstrate is threefold:

1. A genuine good-faith effort to recruit women and minorities. (Good faith does not mean calling one's white male colleague, asking if he knows a good man, and then after the hiring is completed, saying, "Certainly I'd have been glad to hire a qualified woman or minority person if I could have found one. Unfortunately, none applied.")

2. Specification of job-related objective criteria, before the hiring process. The criteria for professional jobs are often complex and difficult to assess; nevertheless, they are subject to the same requirements as other jobs. Subjective, intuitive judgments are not acceptable criteria. For example, the courts have held that promotional policies for executives are subject to standards of objectivity and must be job-related. [3]

3. Equal application of criteria. Whatever standards or criteria are set for white men must be applied equally to women and minorities.

AUTONOMY AND "PREFERENCE"

Some administrators claim that an institution's autonomy is threatened by having numerical goals, and that academic freedom will be violated because they will be "forced" to give "preference" to unqualified women and minorities. Traditionally, academic freedom has meant the right to publish, to teach, and to work with controversial ideas. The aim of numerical goals is not to give preference, but to end preference, the existing preference for males, the existing preference for members of the "old boy" club. Academia has traditionally operated with an unwritten, but functionally effective, "affirmative action" plan for white males. That preference system is now illegal. In one sense, the words "academic freedom" have become a rallying cry and smokescreen to obscure basic issues. Some women's groups claim that they are analogous to the cry of "states rights" and "quality education."

Academia has generally relied on the "old boy" method of recruiting and hiring—the vast, informal network of old school chums, colleagues, drinking buddies—a network to which women and minorities rarely have had access. The merit system has always been a closed merit system, for large portions of the available qualified pool have been excluded. The government is not asking that the merit

---

*There often is a covert assumption that women and minorities are by definition "not qualified."

system be abolished, but only that it be opened up to a larger pool of qualified persons. To recruit in a different manner means additional work and effort, and, more important, it means change. Change is never easy, particularly when it is perceived as a threat to the power base.

Employers in academic institutions have never had to specify criteria for hiring and promotion. Now, when evidence of discrimination is found, the government is asking for an explanation why Mr. X is a full professor and Ms. Y is only a lecturer although she has been given the "best teacher" award and has a string of publications and awards.[4] The government does not set the criteria for hiring and promotion; academic freedom would be violated if it attempted to do so. Institutions and/or department heads should develop their own criteria. What the government does ask is why someone was hired or not hired, and whether the criteria are objective and job-related. Some administrators who have never had to specify criteria understandably feel threatened when asked to do this; however, an administrator who cannot justify an employment decision is very likely to have made a wrong decision or to be an incompetent administrator.

It is quite likely that universities, under numerical goals and affirmative action, will find that the quality of academic appointments will actually improve.* Despite claims of an unbiased objective merit system, academic judgments have too often been intuitive and subjective. Now, instead of being able to justify a candidate merely by saying "he's a well-known and respected scholar," department heads will not only have to develop specific criteria, but will also have to be able to demonstrate that the candidate is the very best person recruited from the largest pool possible, one that includes qualified women and minorities.

Some institutions mistakenly feel that they are now forced to hire women and minorities in order to "get HEW off their back." Decisions based on such a gross misinterpretation of the law are tragic. If institutions give preference to a less-qualified woman or minority person over a better-qualified white male, then such institutions are violating the very laws and regulations they are seeking to observe, because such preferences are clearly prohibited by law. Institutions cannot discriminate against qualified members of any group on the basis of race, color, religion,** national origin, or sex—and this includes discrimination against white males.

---

*Women's groups contend that most of the deadwood that exists on the campus is predominantly white and male.

**However, Title VII of the Civil Rights Act allows religious institutions to give preference to members of their religion in employment. 42 U.S.C. §2000e-1 (1970).

What is not at stake is the hiring of less-qualified persons or "reverse discrimination" but, rather, a very real economic threat: for every woman or minority person who is hired, one less white male is hired. If more women are paid commensurately with their positions, then some men may get raises more slowly or perhaps not at all. It will be harder for qualified white males to get jobs when they compete with qualified women or minorities, but it cannot be termed "reverse discrimination."

TITLE VII OF THE CIVIL RIGHTS ACT OF 1964

Title VII was amended on March 24, 1972, to cover educational institutions. It forbids discrimination in employment and applies to all institutions, public or private, whether or not they receive any federal funds. Title VII is enforced by the Equal Employment Opportunity Commission, which is appointed by the President. As under the executive order, individual charges, as well as charges of a pattern of discrimination, can be filed. However, unlike the executive order, no affirmative action is required; employers are required merely not to discriminate in employment. A conciliation agreement or court order may require affirmative action, but this would be after charges are filed. Unlike under the executive order, Title VII investigations generally are conducted only if charges have been filed.

Should conciliation fail, the Equal Employment Opportunity Commission can take an employer to court.[5] This new provision strengthens EEOC's positions and should speed up the conciliation process considerably. Currently, EEOC has a backlog of several thousand cases, and it sometimes takes a year or two before an investigation is started. (HEW is also backlogged, and a similar period may elapse before a case is investigated.) Recently HEW and EEOC agreed that all individual cases filed with HEW under the executive order after March 24, 1972, will be forwarded to EEOC for investigation and action.

EEOC's sex discrimination guidelines issued on April 5, 1972, are in many ways similar to those issued by the Office of Federal Contract Compliance and HEW, but have stricter provisions in some instances. For example, EEOC requires that the part of maternity leave where a woman is temporarily disabled and cannot work for medical reasons (childbirth and complications of pregnancy, in contrast with child-rearing) must be treated like any other temporary disability. The same guidelines call for equal benefits, including retirement benefits. The TIAA retirement plans to which many institutions subscribe, and which now give women who have made identical contributions lower monthly retirement benefits than men, are in violation of EEOC's guidelines.

Title VII also contains an exemption called a "bona fide occupational qualification" ("b.f.o.q."), whereby an employer may legally
limit particular jobs to one sex. The courts have interpreted this
very narrowly; for instance, actress, lingerie fitter, restroom atten-
dant. In one case involving a woman who was refused a job because
she had a preschool child, the court held that being a mother of a pre-
schooler was not a bona fide occupational qualification, and that the
employer would have to prove that all or substantially all women with
preschool children could not do the job.[6]

THE EQUAL PAY ACT OF 1963

In the Educational Amendments Act of 1972 there is a little-noted
section that extends the coverage of the Equal Pay Act of 1963 to executive, administrative, and professional employees, including all
faculty.[7] Unequal pay on the basis of sex is also forbidden by the
executive order and by Title VII; the Equal Pay Act takes on unique
importance because its procedures differ markedly from those of the
executive order and Title VII. First, it is enforced by the Wage and
Hour Division of the Employment Standards Administration of the Department of Labor; and, like the executive order but unlike Title VII,
reviews can be conducted without prior complaint. The Equal Pay
Act was the first sex-discrimination legislation enacted and has been
successful in getting women millions of dollars in back pay.
   One of the major advantages for complainants under the Equal
Pay Act is that the complaint procedure is very informal; unlike Title
VII, which requires a notarized complaint, the Wage and Hour Division will investigate an establishment on the basis of a letter or even
a telephone call. Unlike Title VII and the executive order, where
generally the individual complainant's name is revealed to the employer, the complainant's name is not revealed to the employer under
the Equal Pay Act. In fact, an employer may not even know that his
establishment has been reported; and when a review is conducted, it
is almost always of the entire establishment. (Occasionally, this is
true of EEOC investigations, and is also true of pattern and practice
reviews under the executive order.) After a review is conducted,
if a violation is found, the employer is asked to settle on the spot—
to raise the wages and to pay back pay to the underpaid workers (the
statute of limitations is two years for a nonwillful violation, three
years for a willful violation). Should the employer refuse (and most
do not, as 95 percent of the cases are settled without recourse to
litigation), the Department of Labor is authorized to go to court. Often employers settle not only because they are clearly in violation
of the law but, in addition, court cases involve public disclosure of

the findings; if the case is settled without litigation, the employer's name is not revealed publicly. Currently there is little backlog in equal-pay cases, although this is expected to change as word reaches women in academic circles.

DISCRIMINATION AGAINST STUDENTS

The Comprehensive Manpower Act of October 1971 (amending the Public Health Service Act) was the first law to affect sex discrimination against students. It forbids discriminatory admissions to schools of medicine, veterinary medicine, pharmacy, optometry, dentistry, and other health professions, such as medical technician or X-ray technician. Similar provisions in the Nurse Training Amendments Act will help men gain access to nursing programs. Title IX of the Educational Amendments of 1972[8] (Higher Education Act) is more extensive. Its basic provision is "No person in the United States shall, on the basis of sex, be excluded from participation in, be denied the benefits of, or be subjected to discrimination under any education program or activity receiving Federal Financial assistance."[9] These sex-discrimination provisions are patterned after Title VI of the Civil Rights Act, which forbids discrimination on the basis of race, color, and national origin in all federally assisted programs.*

All institutions, whether public or private, that receive federal monies by way of a grant, loan, or contract (other than a contract of insurance or guaranty) are covered.** There is an admissions exemption for private undergraduate colleges (as well as single-sex public undergraduate institutions), but these institutions are not exempt from the prohibitions of other kinds of discrimination against students because of sex. Discrimination in admissions is specifically prohibited in vocational institutions, professional and graduate institutions, and all public undergraduate coeducational institutions, as are discriminatory practices in athletics, financial aid, and parietal rules.

Individuals and organizations can challenge any discriminatory practice in a federal program or activity by writing the Secretary of HEW, being assured that during the review process, names of complainants are kept confidential, if possible. If violations are found, informal conciliation and persuasion are first used to eliminate the discriminatory practices. Should this fail, formal hearings are con-

---

*Title VI, however, specifically exempts employment from coverage. Title IX has no such exemption. Discrimination against employees on the basis of sex is therefore covered by Title IX.

**This includes preschools, elementary, and secondary schools.

ducted and federal assistance can be terminated. HEW's Office for
Civil Rights will be the enforcement agency for these provisions. Implementing regulations will detail the procedures for the Act.[10]

SIMULTANEOUS FILING

The application of the Equal Pay Act and Title VII to faculty, as
well as Title IX to employees and students, is, of course, very new.
Some women's groups have begun to file complaints under Equal Pay,
Title VII, the executive order, and Title IX simultaneously. At this
point, under the executive order alone the number of sex-discrimination complaints against universities and colleges exceeds that of those
filed by all minorities.

COURT DECISIONS

Despite some overlapping coverage, the principles utilized by
the separate federal agencies to determine policies regarding discrimination are similar. The Office of Federal Contract Compliance,
as well as the other agencies, continually examines court decisions
concerning discrimination, and uses them as a solid base for determining policy.*

Many of the issues now being debated, somewhat ex post facto,
in the Halls of Ivy have already been decided in the courts.

Court decisions that were previously applicable to discrimination
in nonacademic settings now extend to the educational world. Most of
these have occurred in cases involving race, but the principles essentially extend to other minority groups, including women. Among
those likely to have the most impact are the following:

_____

*With the exception of maternity and retirement benefits, federal
policy is remarkably uniform among the several agencies. Differences in investigative and administrative procedures are far greater
and more likely to cause difficulties with regard to institutions. Section 715 of the Equal Employment Act of 1972 created a committee
composed of the Secretary of Labor, the chairman of the Equal Employment Opportunity Commission, the Attorney General, and chairman of the U.S. Commission on Civil Rights that is authorized to develop "agreements, policies, and procedures designed to maximize
effort, promote efficiency and eliminate conflict, competition, dupli-
cation and inconsistency."

1. The existence of intent to discriminate is irrelevant. The effect of a policy or practice is what counts, rather than intent or lack of intent.[11] (Even the best-intentioned may often unknowingly act in a discriminatory manner.)

2. Statistics can be used to document a pattern of discrimination. Indeed, statistics can be used as prima facie evidence of discrimination. "Statistics often tell much, and courts listen."[12] The courts have not hesitated to use statistics both as a measure of discrimination and as a measure of compliance. Institutions cannot rebut statistical evidence on the basis that no women or minorities applied. (An institution may have a reputation as discriminatory, and that may have had a "chilling" effect on employment applications.)[13] When statistical evidence indicates that there has been a pattern of discrimination, the burden of proof is shifted to the employer, who must demonstrate that there is, and has been, no discrimination;[14] that the job criteria are indeed job-related; and that employment practices do not, and have not had, a discriminatory effect.

3. Any individual, including a third party, has standing to raise class allegations and charge a pattern of discrimination, using statistics as evidence.[15] Persons can make a general allegation of discrimination without having to name names and incidents.[16] The appropriate federal agency then investigates to see if the charges are substantiated.

4. All hiring and promotion policies must be based on objective, job-related criteria.[17] For example, a promotion policy that is not job-related, and that is implemented by predominantly white males, can be held to be discriminatory.[18] Positive empirical evidence, and not the subjective opinion of supervisors, is necessary to establish a good defense against a charge of discrimination.[19]

5. Professional employment is not exempt from the requirement of having objective and job-related criteria.[20] Employers also have a duty of fair recruitment.[21] If an administrator ends up with only white males, where there is a pool of qualified women and minorities available, the institution may well be discriminating and may be called upon to prove that it is not.

6. Any policy or practice that has an adverse or disparate effect on a protected class (women and minorities), and cannot be justified by business necessity, is considered discriminatory. The United States Supreme Court, with the majority opinion written by Chief Justice Burger, enunciated this principle in the landmark decision in Griggs vs. Duke Power Co.[22]

The Griggs doctrine suggests word-of-mouth hiring as a policy that appears to be fair on its face, but is nevertheless discriminatory in its impact because women and minorities are largely excluded from the "old boy" network. Similarly, policies of nepotism or practices

that apply to "spouse" may also appear to be fair in form; but when
their effect is predominantly felt by women, they violate the law.
Age requirements, and restrictions on part-time employment and on
part-time studies, will probably come under increasing scrutiny because they also tend to have a disparate effect on women.

7. Motherhood by itself is not a rational basis for exclusion,
and marital status must not be considered in employment decisions.[23]
Whether or not a woman is married cannot enter into a job decision,
unless the same criteria are applied equally to men. A woman cannot
be paid less because she is or is not married.

8. Seniority systems, such as tenure, that have been discriminatory may come under review if they perpetuate the effects of prior discriminatory hiring and promotion practices because they have the effect of "freezing an entire generation."[24] Termination of women who
do not have tenure because of prior discrimination may well be illegal.

9. Attorney's fees are authorized for complainants under Title
VII and have also been awarded in at least one HEW case arising under Executive Order 11246 as amended. Punitive damages have also
been awarded in numerous civil rights cases and in at least one case
under Title VII.[25] Back pay can also be awarded under numerous
federal laws and regulations[26] prohibiting discrimination, and may
include interest.

10. Preference of employees for white or male coworkers or
supervisors is not relevant for hiring decisions. Such practices
might have a disparate effect on women and minorities, and would be
difficult to justify either as a bona fide occupational qualification or
on the basis of business necessity.[27]

Equal pay for equal work does not necessarily mean identical
work, but only substantially equal work. Insubstantial differences
are to be ignored; what is considered important are the job requirements as a whole, and not paying women less simply because they often command a lower market value.[28] The law does not prohibit bona
fide differences in pay based on merit or seniority; however, such a
system cannot be based on either sex or race.

11. Numerical goals have been upheld and ordered by the courts
in numerous discrimination cases. Individuals must also be considered on the basis of individual capacities and not on the basis of any
characteristics attributed to the group.[29] The fact that some or even
many women are thought to be unable to do a particular job is not a
justification for excluding all women; it is not a justification for a
bona fide occupational qualification.

GOALS VS. QUOTAS

The courts have clearly distinguished between numerical goals
and preference in numerous cases, and have upheld goals as a permis-

sible method of redressing past inequities.[30] Civil rights legislation
is intimately related to the equitable concept of "setting things right"
that is the guiding principle underlying numerical goals. The court
"may order such affirmative relief as may be appropriate. [It] has
not merely the power, but the duty to render a decree which so far
as possible [will] eliminate the discriminatory effects of the past as
well as bar like discrimination in the future."[31] (Emphasis added.)

The courts have consistently established the principle that when
the proportion of minorities is less than would be expected on the basis of qualified minority members available, there is a presumption
of discrimination. The burden is then shifted to the employer to demonstrate that such underutilization is not a product of discrimination.[32]
Underutilization, under existing case law, raises a presumption of
discrimination under the executive order, Title VII, and other legislation.

Goals are set only after there has been a finding of discrimination, and they have been upheld in the courts as relief for a substantiated pattern of discrimination. The aim is not punitive; no one is
required to be fired. Goals are simply an attempt to remedy the continued effect of discrimination in the present, and to give relief to a
specific class that has been discriminated against in the past.

Under the executive order, the contractor does its own self-anal-
ysis of underutilization and develops its own goals. In contrast, under Title VII (as well as in cases under the Fifth or Fourteenth Amendments) it is the government that does the analysis; and upon a finding
of discrimination, it is the government and/or the courts that set
the numerical or percentage goals. The goal is tailored to a particular discriminatory situation. If it were not, it would violate the equal
protection of white males. The goal is generally developed in terms
of anticipated employee turnover rate, rate of new hires, promotion
and upgrading, and the availability of qualified women and minorities,
not the number or proportion of women and minorities in the population. The numerical goal often varies for different job classifications,
and within institutions it could vary from department to department.
The courts have also clearly maintained that affirmative action and
goals are not preferential treatment when undertaken to remedy past
discriminatory practices. They are not totally unsympathetic to the
problems of white males (who will probably find it harder now that
they must compete with women and minorities) but have felt that the
more important concern was for the victims of discrimination: "Adequate protection of Negro* rights under Title VII may necessitate . . .

---

*The same principle applies equally to women and other minority
groups.

some adjustment of the rights of white employees. The Court must be free to deal equitably with conflicting interests of white employees in order to shape remedies that will effectively protect and redress the rights of Negro victims of discrimination."[33]

All of the court cases involving numerical or percentage goals have two things in common: the goals are enacted for a limited time or until they are achieved and the effect of past discrimination is corrected;[34] and there is no compulsion to hire unqualified persons to meet the goal. In the few cases where goals have been overturned by the courts, it was because the goal was not a goal but a quota, and because there was no provision to insure that qualified persons were hired.[35]

LOOKING AHEAD: INCREASED LITIGATION

Women's groups can be expected to use the courts with increasing frequency, particularly with the extension of Title VII to cover educational institutions. About 250 institutions had charges filed against them under Title VII during the first year of coverage.

The Equal Employment Opportunity Commission can take to court employers who are found to be in violation of Title VII, although in most instances it is expected that employers will negotiate out-of-court conciliation agreements. Moreover, Title VII also allows individuals the right to file private suits against employers, thus allowing them to avoid the long delay of an EEOC investigation. The University of Pittsburgh has the dubious distinction of being the first academic institution to have a private lawsuit filed under these provisions, with the result that a preliminary injunction has stopped it from firing a woman faculty member.[36]

Under the executive order, about 500 institutions have been charged with a pattern and practice of sex discrimination, with some of these institutions being simultaneously filed against under Title VII. About 250 individual cases have also been filed with HEW.

Numerous complaints of unequal pay have been investigated by the Equal Pay Division of the Department of Labor. Because of the anonymity features of Equal Pay enforcement and the informality of the complaint process, it is difficult to determine the number of complaints actually "filed" under the Equal Pay Act, although the number seems close to several hundred. Other cases have been filed under the Fourteenth Amendment and Section 1933 of the Civil Rights Act of 1866. None of these have been settled as yet, but among the institutions being sued are the University of California at Berkeley, the University of Maryland, Florida State University, the University of Pittsburgh, and Texas Tech University.[37] Some of these suits in-

volve requests for back pay and damages of more than a million dollars. Numerous others are in preparation, and still others have been
filed under various state and local human relations laws.

The Department of Justice may also become involved in cases concerning educational institutions.* It can take cases directly to the
courts, and has already done so in noneducational private and public
employment cases. It can also act on cases sent directly to it, although most cases reach it via other governmental enforcement agencies. The department can entertain all cases involving patterns and
practices of discrimination, as well as individual cases suggesting
them. (In those individual cases that do not suggest a pattern, but
are isolated instances of discrimination, the Department of Justice
can only handle them where the employee is employed by a public institution and the case has been referred to it by EEOC.)

In the years to come the academic community is likely to be beset
by a variety of issues. Although the financial crisis is likely to be
the first issue of concern, sex discrimination will probably be the
second largest. The impact will be enormous, for many of the traditional practices and policies of academia will come under increasing
fire for their discriminatory effect on women and minorities. Women
are the fastest-growing and potentially the largest advocacy group on
campus. They are challenging policies and practices, and using the
law to its full extent. The hand that rocked the cradle has learned to
rock the boat.

NOTES

1. P.L. no. 92-261 §2, 86 Stat. 103, amending 42 U.S.C. §2000e-1
(1970); P.L. no. 92-318, Title IX, §906(b)(1), 86 Stat. 373, June 23,
1972; P.L. no. 92-157§110, 85 Stat. 431, amending 42 U.S.C.A.
§295h-9; P.L. no. 92-318, Title IX, §901, 86 Stat. 373, June 23,
1972. (Private undergraduate institutions and public single-sex
schools are exempt from the nondiscriminatory admissions provisions,
but there can be no discrimination on the basis of sex against students in such institutions once they have been admitted.); P.L. no.
92-496§3, 86 Stat. 813, amending 42 U.S.C.A.§1975c(a)(1957).

2. Statement of Affirmative Action for Equal Employment Opportunities by the U.S. Commission on Civil Rights, U.S. Commission
on Civil Rights, 1973, p. 14.

---

*The 1972 amendments to Title VII provide that the authority of
the Department of Justice to bring suit against private employers
will be transferred to EEOC after March 24, 1974.

3. Marquez vs. Ford Motor Co., Omaha District Sales Office, 440 F.2d 1157 (8th Cir. 1971).

4. This example is based on an actual incident in an HEW review. The source is confidential.

5. P.L. no. 92-496, 3, 86 Stat. 813, amending 42 U.S.L.A. 1975c(a)(1957).

6. Phillips vs. Martin-Marietta Corp., 400 U.S. 542 (1971). Although the woman involved was white, the NAACP took on the case because it saw the implications for black women as well.

7. P.L. no. 92-318, Title IX, §906(b)(1), 86 Stat. 373, June 23, 1972.

8. Ibid.

9. Ibid.

10. Proposed regulations were published in the Federal Register, 39, no. 120, Pt. II (June 20, 1974): 22227-40.

11. Griggs vs. Duke Power Co., 401 U.S. 424 (1971).

12. State of Alabama vs. United States, 304 F.2d 583 (5th Cir. 1962), aff'd mem., 371 U.S. 37 (1962). See also Jones vs. Lee Way Motor Freight, Inc., 431 F.2d 245 (19th Cir. 1970), cert. denied, 401 U.S. 423 (1971), rehearing denied 401 U.S. 1014 (1971); Carter vs. Gallagher, 452 F.2d 315 (8th Cir. 1971), cert. denied, 406 U.S. 950 (1972); Parham vs. Southwestern Bell Telephone Co., 433 F.2d 421 (8th Cir. 1970).

13. Lea vs. Cone Mills, 301 F. Supp 97 (M.D.N.C. 1969); Cypress vs. Newport News General and Non-Sectarian Hospital Assoc., 375 F.2d 648 (4th Cir. 1967).

14. United States vs. United Brotherhood of Carpenters and Joiners, Local 169, 457 F.2d 210, 214 (7th Cir. 1972).

15. Jenkins vs. United Gas Corp., 400 F.2d 28 (5th Cir. 1968); Bowe vs. Colgate-Palmolive, 416 F.2a 711 (7th Cir. 1969).

16. Graniteville Co., Sibley Div., vs. EEOC, 438 F.2d 32 (4th Cir. 1971).

17. Griggs vs. Duke Power Co., 401 U.S. 424 (1971).

18. Rowe vs. General Motors Corp., 457 F.2d 348 (5th Cir. 1972).

19. United States vs. Jacksonville Terminal, 451 F.2d 418 (5th Cir. 1971).

20. Marquez vs. Ford Motor Co., Omaha District Sales Office, 440 F.2d 1157 (8th Cir. 1971).

21. United States vs. Plumbers, Local 73, 314 F. Supp. 160 (S.D. Ind. 1969); Asbestos Workers, Local 53 vs. Vogler, 407 F.2d 1047 (5th Cir. 1969); Parham vs. Southwestern Bell, 433 F.2d 421 (8th Cir. 1970); Lea vs. Cone Mills, 301 F. Supp. 97 (M.D.N.C. 1969).

22. 401 U.S. 424 (1971).

23. See discussion, Phillips vs. Martin-Marietta Corp., 400 U.S. 542 (1971). Also see Sprogis vs. United Airlines, 444 F.2d 1194 (7th Cir. 1971); Doe vs. Osteopathic Hospital of Wichita, Inc., 333 F. Supp. 1357 (D. Kan. 1971).

24. Quarles vs. Philip Morris, Inc., 279 F. Supp. 505 (E.D. Va. 1968); Hicks vs. Crown Zellerbach Corp., 319 F. Supp. 314 (E.D. La. 1970); Local 189, United Papermakers, vs. United States, 416 F.2d 980 (5th Cir. 1969), cert. denied, 397 U.S. 919 (1970).

25. Evans vs. Sheraton Park Hotel, 5 F.E.P. 393 (D.D.C. 1972).

26. Title VII of the Civil Rights Act and the Equal Pay Act of 1964. Back pay has also been awarded in at least one HEW case under Executive Order 11246 as amended.

27. Griggs vs. Duke Power Co., 401 U.S. 424 (1971). See also Diaz vs. Pan American Airways, Inc., 442 F.2d 385 (5th Cir. 1971).

28. Shultz vs. Brookhaven Central General Hospital, 305 F. Supp. 424 (N.D. Tex., 1969).

29. Weeks vs. Southern Bell Telephone and Telegraph Co., 408 F.2d 228 (5th Cir. 1969).

30. For a lengthy, but only partial, list of cases, see Technical Comment #1, International Association of Official Human Rights Agencies, 1625 K St., N.W., Washington, D.C. 20006, September 7, 1972. Upon appeal, the Supreme Court has let all of these decisions stand by denying certiorari.

31. Louisiana vs. United States, 380 U.S. 145, 154 (1965).

32. For a list of cases see Statement of Affirmative Action for Equal Employment Opportunities by the U.S. Commission on Civil Rights, U.S. Commission on Civil Rights, 1973, p. 6.

33. Vogler vs. McCarty, Inc., 451 F.2d 1236, 1238 (5th Cir. 1971).

34. Carter vs. Gallagher, 452 F.2d 315 (8th Cir. 1971): "Such a procedure does not constitute a 'quota' system, because as soon as the trial court's order is fully implemented, all hiring will be on a racially non-discriminatory basis, and it could well be that many more minority persons or less, as compared to the total population at large, over a period of time would apply and qualify for the position." At 330-31.

35. See the 3rd Circuit decision overturning part of the order by the U.S. District Court in the Eastern District of Pennsylvania involving the hiring of policemen. Commonwealth of Pennsylvania vs. O'Neil. 473 F.2d 1029 (1973). "This order does not, certainly on its face, limit the pool from which applicants are to be chosen to those necessarily qualified to be policemen."

36. Johnson vs. University of Pittsburgh, 359 F. Supp. 1002 (W.D. Pa. 1973).

37. League of Academic Women vs. Regents of University of California, 343 F. Supp. 636 (N.D. Calif., 1972); Cussler vs. University of Maryland, no. 72-372 (D.C. April 13, 1972); Menzel vs. Florida State University, no. TCA 1834 (N.D. Fla. June 1972); Braden vs. University of Pittsburgh, 343 F. Supp. 836 (1972), vacated remanded, 477 F.2d I (3rd Cir. 1973); Green vs. Board of Regents of Texas Tech. Univ., 474 F. 2d 594 (5th Cir. 1973).

4

RACE, SEX,
AND JOBS:
THE DRIVE
TOWARD EQUALITY
J. Stanley Pottinger

About two years ago, a previously unnoticed executive order prohibiting employment discrimination by federal contractors (which includes most universities) was discovered by women's organizations
and minority groups on a few East Coast campuses. Soon afterward
the volume of formal complaints of sex and race employment discrimination in institutions of higher education rose sharply, and the Office
for Civil Rights began constructing a systematic program of enforcement. During the early stages of this process, as the Office struggled
to define law and policy and to obtain staff, the attention and support
of women's and civil rights groups increased, while the higher education establishment remained unruffled.

When the Office made its presence on campuses felt, however—
by deferring payment of some $23 million in federal contracts to
various universities pending compliance with the order—it began to
raise the academic community's eyebrows. Today a significant and
vocal segment of that community is actively challenging HEW's enforcement of Executive Order 11246 and the policies upon which it is
based.

THE QUOTA ISSUE

The reasons for this challenge are, as one might expect, more
complex than the current dialogue on the subject would suggest. But
every crusade must have its simplistic side—a galvanizing symbol, a

---

*Reprinted with permission from Change 4, no. 8.

bogeyman, a rallying cry. The word "quotas" serves these rhetori-
cal purposes in the present case. Since quotas are not required or
permitted by the executive order, they are for the most part a phony
issue, but very much an issue nevertheless.

To understand the quotas issue, one must first understand what
the executive order is all about. In attempting to deal with employment inequities, Executive Order 11246 embodies two concepts: nondiscrimination and affirmative action.

Nondiscrimination means the elimination of all existing discriminatory treatment of present and potential employees. University officials are required, under this concept, to ensure that their employment policies do not, if followed as stated, operate to the detriment
of any persons on grounds of race, color, religion, sex, or national
origin. Typically, this means eliminating officially sanctioned quotas
restricting women and minorities, antinepotism policies that operate
to deny equal opportunities to women, recruitment procedures that
tend exclusively to reach white males, and the like. In addition, the
university must examine the practices of its decision-makers to ensure that nondiscriminatory policies are in fact implemented in a
nondiscriminatory way. This may require warning or firing personnel who, for example, reject women's applications not on the basis
of merit, but (as we have found) with a cursory note that "we have
enough of these" or "sorry, but we have filled our women's quota"—
despite the fact that quotas or discriminatory policies are not official
policy.

The concept of affirmative action requires more than mere neutrality on race and sex. It requires the university to determine
whether it has failed to recruit, employ, and promote women and
minorities commensurate with their availability, even if this failure
cannot be traced to specific acts of discrimination by university officials. Where women and minorities are not represented on a university's rolls, despite their availability (that is, where they are "underutilized"), the university has an obligation to initiate affirmative efforts to recruit and hire them. The premise of this obligation is
that systemic forms of exclusion, inattention, and discrimination cannot be remedied in any meaningful way, in any reasonable length of
time, simply by ensuring a future benign neutrality with regard to
race and sex. This would indefinitely perpetuate the grossest inequities of past discrimination. Thus there must be some form of positive action, along with a schedule for how such action is to take place,
and an honest appraisal of what the plan is likely to yield—an appraisal that the regulations call a "goal."

It is at this point that the issue of "quotas" rears its ugly head.
What is a quota, and what is wrong with it? What is a goal, and what
is right about it?

Historically, hiring quotas have been rigid numerical ceilings on the number of persons of a given racial, ethnic, religious, or sex group who could be employed by (or admitted to) an academic institution. If quotas were required or permitted by the executive order, they would operate as levels of employment that must be fulfilled if the university is to remain eligible for federal contracts.

Some critics have assumed that the government is arguing that rigid numerical requirements would not constitute quotas under the executive order, since, unlike traditional quotas, they would operate in favor of minorities and women rather than against them. But obviously, where the number of jobs is finite, as is true in all universities, a numerical requirement in favor of any group becomes by definition a restrictive ceiling or quota for all others. No one in the government is making an argument that any requirements in the form of quotas—for or against a defined class—are legitimate.

Once it is assumed that quotas are required, of course, there is no end to the horrors and hysteria that can be generated. University officials, it is said, will be obliged to hire regardless of merit or capability. Standards of excellence will crumble. Existing faculty will be fired and replaced wholesale. And if there are not enough qualified women engineers to fill the engineering department's quota, never mind; the positions will be filled with female home economics teachers (a favorite stereotype), and don't blame the university if the country's next suspension bridge looks like a plate of spaghetti. If there are not enough black surgeons to teach surgery, no matter; they'll be hired anyway, and when scores of hapless patients (hopefully Office for Civil Rights personnel) are left bleeding on the table, don't come to the universities for so much as a Band-Aid. If there are not enough qualified Chicano professors of Latin and Greek to fill their quotas, Latin and Greek can be dropped from the curriculum, and don't blame the universities for the fall of Western civilization.

Perhaps these charges would be worthy of debate if quotas were required. But they are not. Department of Labor guidelines state that goals "may not be rigid and inflexible quotas that must be met." HEW directives reflect the same policy. Furthermore, the executive order is a presidential directive, and the President's prohibition of quotas is clear: "With respect to . . . Affirmative Action programs, I agree that numerical goals, although an important and useful tool to measure progress which remedies the effect of past discrimination, must not be allowed to be applied in such a fashion as to, in fact, result in the imposition of quotas."

GOALS AND GOOD FAITH EFFORTS

What is required by the executive order is evidence of good faith and a positive effort to recruit and hire women and minorities. Since the road to exclusively white male faculties is paved with good intentions, however, we ask for something more than the mere promise of good behavior. Universities are required to commit themselves to defined, specific steps that will bring them into contact with qualified women and minorities and that will ensure that in the selection process they will be judged fairly, on the basis of their capabilities. Universities are also required to make an honest prediction of what these efforts are likely to yield over a given period of time, assuming that the availability of women and minorities is accurately estimated and assuming that the procedures for recruitment and selection are actually followed.

This predictive aspect of affirmative action could be called any number of things: "level of expectancy," "honest guesses," "targets." It happens to be called "goals." The important point is not the term, but how it functions. Unlike quotas, goals are not the sole measure of a contractor's compliance. Good-faith efforts and adherence to procedures that are likely to yield results remain the test of compliance. A university, in other words, would be required to make precisely the same level of effort, set and adhere to the same procedures, and take the same steps to correct the lack of women and minorities resulting from former exclusion, even if goals and timetables did not exist at all.

If goals are not designed to warp affirmative action toward quotas, what is the purpose of requiring them at all? There are two reasons.

First, since a university cannot predict employment results in the form of goals without first analyzing its deficiencies and determining what steps are likely to remedy them, the setting of goals serves as an inducement to lay the analytical foundation necessary to guarantee nondiscrimination and the affirmative efforts required by the executive order.

Second, goals serve as one way of measuring a university's level of effort. If a university falls short of its goals at the end of a given period, that failure in itself does not require a conclusion of noncompliance (as would be the case if quotas were in use). It does, however, signal to the university that something has gone awry, and that reasons for the failure should be examined. If it appears, for example, that the cause for failure was not a lack of defined effort or adherence to fair procedures, then we regard compliance to have taken place. Perhaps the university's original goals were unrealistically high in light of later job market conditions. Or perhaps it faced an unforeseen contraction of its employment positions, or similar conditions beyond its control. On the other hand, if the failure to reach goals was clearly a failure to abide by the affirmative action program set by the university, compliance is an issue, and a hearing is likely to ensue.

Once it is understood that there is nothing in the executive order that requires quotas, it should be equally clear that there is nothing that requires their undesirable side effects either. White males or other allegedly "overrepresented" groups should not be fired in order to permit goal fulfillment; indeed, to do so would constitute a violation of law. Standards of performance and qualifications that are not themselves discriminatory need not be abandoned or compromised in order to hire unqualified women and minorities. (The argument frequently advanced by university officials that there are virtually no qualified women and minorities who are currently unemployed or unpromoted simply does not stand up, particularly when advanced by universities that have failed even to canvass the market.) Nothing in the affirmative action concept infringes on "academic freedom" or the university's right to teach, research, or publish whatever it wishes, in whatever forum it desires—whether the classroom, the laboratory, the campus, the press, or elsewhere.

If goals are not quotas, and quotas really are not required, why the current fuss and confusion?

The Office for Civil Rights must share some of the blame for not getting the distinction between quotas and goals firmly and early implanted in the higher education community. But such efforts have not been lacking in the last year. The distinction has been drawn repeatedly in press releases, speeches, letters to editors, articles, compliance reviews, and negotiations. Indeed, the effort has been so substantial that a cynical observer might be inclined to conclude that at least some of the academic community, priding itself as it does on careful research and the intellectual ability to comprehend important distinctions, hears us loud and clear but simply does not want to understand. The Memorandum to College and University Presidents dated December 1974 from the Director of the Office for Civil Rights of the Department of Health, Education, and Welfare should help to resolve the quota controversy once and for all.

Some critics object to goals not because they fail to understand how they differ from quotas, or because they secretly want to throttle effort-oriented affirmative action. They object to the use of goals because of their fear that sound conceptual distinctions will be lost; and in actual practice, goals will be used as quotas, regardless of the law.

THE "REVERSE DISCRIMINATION" CHARGE

No one would agree more quickly than I that this form of "affirmative action with a vengeance" is an outrageous and illegal form of reverse bias. I am not ready to agree, however, that blame for this

petulant behavior must be laid to goals, or that valid distinctions between goals and quotas are too elusive for university officials to follow
if they are sharply interested in equal opportunity.

More than once, we have discovered that what appears to be reverse discrimination born of a confusion about quotas is really nothing more than avoidance of a decision on the merits. A white male is
told that he was the "top candidate" for the job, when in fact that is
not the truth. The personnel officer, lacking the fortitude to reject
the applicant honestly, and shaking his head in mock sympathetic dis-
gust, conveniently delivers the bad news as "federally required reverse discrimination."

But even if some employment decision-makers engage in reverse
discrimination out of an honest mistake about what is required, the
concept of goals should not be abandoned by way of overreaction, at
least not while so many questions remain unanswered. When reverse
discrimination is discovered on the campus, why should the academic
community immediately assume that the federal government is the
villain? The Office for Civil Rights is remote from the actual hiring
process, and rightly so, while the university department head is right
where the action is. The scant efforts by top university officials to
correct abuses or to educate their colleagues to the real issues at
stake in carrying out affirmative action cast doubt on the credibility
of their protestations.

One also needs to ask just how widespread reverse discrimination
really is. Evidence suggests that there may be some loosening of
high school academic achievement scores with regard to the admission of disadvantaged students to undergraduate colleges. The merits
of this policy aside, it has nothing to do with employment standards
under the executive order; and there is no clear evidence that goals
or affirmative action requirements are prompting widespread abuses
in the employment process.

But even if the problem is widespread, or likely to become so,
assuming that goals are the problem still misses the point. If, as
our critics seem to imply, numbers of faculty and administrators are
truly incapable of understanding and adhering to the distinction between a goal and a quota, or willfully commit reverse discrimination,
are we ready to believe that these people will behave differently if
goals are removed? To make the point that goals cannot operate in
the real world without becoming quotas, critics must characterize
university officials generally as ignorant, as spiteful, as unconcerned
about merit, or as weaklings ready to collapse in the face of supposed
whispered directions "from upstairs" to hire unqualified women and
minorities because that is the easiest way to ensure a flow of federal
dollars. It is an unconscionable argument and an unfair condemna-
tion of the academics' intelligence and integrity.

There is yet another fear: even if goals are not converted to quotas by university officials, they may be by the government. As a prominent newspaper editor said recently, "The distinction between goals and quotas may be sound today, but how do we know that in the future a different Director of Civil Rights will not tack goals to the university door and proclaim them to be quotas?" The short answer is that we do not know. No one can guarantee today that tomorrow's government officials will never exceed the bounds of good policy or legitimate discretion. This possibility exists in virtually every government program, but we also enjoy adequate due process safeguards in the courts, as well as a constant vigilance by the Congress and the President.

Hindsight has shown on more than one occasion that an unsuccessful program that seemed right at its inception should never have been launched. But it is equally true that most policies that turn out to have dealt successfully with controversial issues also faced extinction at the outset because of someone's fear that they might "get out of hand" and should therefore be "nipped in the bud." The historical observation that these possibilities exist gives little help in determining whether abuses are so widespread that the policy in question presents a greater evil than the one to be remedied.

Unfortunately, it is my impression that some critics who argue that goals are quotas are really not arguing against quotas at all. They understand the distinction between the two, and they understand that one need not inevitably become the other. Their insistence on crying "quota" to every discussion on affirmative action, and their refusal to accompany their arguments with any alternatives that would appear to guarantee affirmative action without goals, lead to the conclusion that their real target is affirmative action itself.

Too many university spokesmen are in this position today. A university's salary analysis, for instance, may reveal significant discrepancies in pay to white men, minority men, white women, and minority women in the same job classification, doing the same work. The issue has nothing to do with quotas, yet the university refuses to make the analysis or salary adjustments without a protracted struggle with HEW and the risk of deferring important contracts.

Attention to such matters as fair and adequate grievance procedures, antinepotism regulations, salary reviews and adjustments, training for nonacademic personnel, safeguards against "clustering" or segregation of women, Chicanos, Jews, or others, guarantees of nondiscriminatory leave policies for men and women—have no bearing on hiring or promotion policies, goals, or quotas. Yet too many institutions are still failing to deal with them voluntarily. Instead, facile objections are raised to all affirmative action as constituting reverse discrimination and preferential treatment. And since these phrases ordinarily imply the evils of "quotas," the criticisms, no matter how simplistic or irrelevant, slide easily into a rhetorically appealing "anti-quota" posture.

The pathetic irony about those who say "never" to employment policy changes is the certainty with which they are inviting the very federal presence that they and their colleagues deplore. Historically, universities throughout the country have understandably resisted government intervention in even the most trivial aspects of university life, to keep out influence over their teaching, research, publication, and curricula. At the same time, however, there cannot be a university or college anywhere in the country today that does not know that where basic grievances exist, those who are aggrieved will turn to every available source for redress, including the federal government. And surely they must know that if the university does not voluntarily deal with the issue, a vacuum is created that the government, like nature, abhors. Knowing this, it is deeply troubling to see the lethargy and paralysis with which so many universities have responded to even the most fundamental grievances presented.

For those who agree that affirmative action is necessary and appropriate, and that goals are conceptually consistent with that approach, what is needed desperately today is an effort at the university level to make affirmative action work. If this occurs, both the universities and the government can make sure that affirmative action remains within boundaries that preclude quotas and reverse discrimination.

All of us must recognize that, ultimately, the success of any continuing struggle for equal opportunity depends heavily upon the devotion of our great institutions of higher learning to the protection and extension of human rights and opportunities to everyone. Whether this is recognized as a morally compelling argument or as a way to avoid the potentially corrosive effects of federal involvement matters little, as long as the result is to deal with the problems of exclusion and discrimination that even our critics do not deny. Let us now move to a mature recognition of the talent of all persons in our society, thereby enriching their lives and that of the university community as well.

5

LEGAL REQUIREMENTS, STRUCTURES, AND STRATEGIES FOR ELIMINATING SEX DISCRIMINATION IN ACADEME

Lenore J. Weitzman

Affirmative action embodies two concepts: the elimination of existing discriminatory conditions and the institution of specific efforts to recruit, employ, and promote qualified women and minorities. As the 1972 "Higher Education Guidelines" issued by the Department of Health, Education and Welfare indicate, it is not enough to eliminate all existing discriminatory conditions, for "unless positive action is undertaken to overcome the effects of systemic institutional forms of exclusion and discrimination, a benign neutrality in employment practices will tend to perpetuate the status quo indefinitely."[1]

This chapter examines specific affirmative action structures and strategies for academic women. The first section highlights legal requirements for an affirmative action plan. Then some structural pitfalls to avoid are reviewed. The third section suggests specific action programs for recruitment, selection, promotion, salary equity, and conditions of employment. It also discusses a monitoring system and sanctions. The fourth section takes us beyond the paper plans and discusses problems of implementation and the effects of unconscious bias. In the fifth and final section, action strategies for academic women are suggested.

Although any complete affirmative action program must deal with both minorities and women, and with both academic and nonaca-

---

Parts of this chapter have appeared in Lenore J. Weitzman, "Affirmative Action Plans for Eliminating Sex Discrimination in Academe," in Alice S. Rossi and Ann Calderwood, eds., Academic Women on the Move (New York: Russell Sage Foundation, 1973). Copyright (C) 1973 Russell Sage Foundation.

demic employees, the most successful programs for each of these groups may differ. My expertise, and this chapter, are restricted to affirmative action for academic women.

THE LEGALLY REQUIRED COMPONENTS OF
AN AFFIRMATIVE ACTION PLAN

Executive Order 11375 requires the elimination of sex discrimination by all federal contractors and a written affirmative action plan from those contractors with $50,000 or more of federal contracts. The ultimate responsibility for enforcing the executive order lies with the Office of Federal Contract Compliance (OFCC) of the Department of Labor. However, OFCC has asked the Department of Health, Education and Welfare (HEW), through its Office for Civil Rights, to enforce the executive order in educational institutions. The discussion of legal requirements for affirmative action in academe that follows refers to the requirements established by both OFCC and HEW. The two most important sets of requirements issued to date are Order no. 4, issued by OFCC in 1971, which establishes the necessary components of affirmative action programs for all federal contractors,[2] and the Higher Education Guidelines issued by HEW in 1972, which interprets the meaning of sections of Order no. 4 for educational institutions.

The eight essential components of an affirmative action program, as outlined in the OFCC and HEW regulations, are presented below.

Maintenance of a Written Affirmative
Action Program

According to OFCC Regulations, §60-2.13a and §60-2.20, and HEW Guidelines, p. 2, all educational institutions, both public and private, are required to maintain a written affirmative action policy and program.

Publication and Dissemination of
the Affirmative Action Program

OFCC Regulations, §60-2.13b and §60.2.21, and HEW Guidelines, pp. 16-17, state that colleges and universities must communicate their affirmative action programs to all persons responsible for their implementation. At a minimum this would include distribution to all faculty members, as most of them are involved in personnel decisions

and must know the institution's program in order to implement it
within their department or school. The 1972 Higher Education Guidelines state that affirmative action plans, once accepted by HEW, are
subject to public disclosure under the Freedom of Information Act
(with the exception that confidential information about employees is
exempt).[3]

Responsibility for Implementing
the Program

A proviso of OFCC Regulations, §60-2.13c and §60-2.22, and
HEW Guidelines, p. 15, is that every educational institution must appoint an administrator to direct its affirmative action program.
This person is responsible for setting up procedures to organize and
monitor the program. He or she is charged with periodic auditing
of all hiring and promotion patterns and with evaluating departmental
progress (including an evaluation of the departmental chairpersons
who have responsibility for implementing the program on the departmental level). In view of this individual's responsibilities as specified in Order no. 4, she or he might be appointed to the top administrative ranks of an institution: as provost or vice-president in a university, as a dean in a college.

Utilization Analysis of Female Employees
by Department and Rank, and
Identification of Problem Areas

Under OFCC Regulations, §60-2.11 and §60-2.23, and HEW
Guidelines, p. 16, "utilization analysis" is the official term for an
examination of the absolute and relative employment of women on
both a departmental and a university basis. It is designed to determine current deficiencies that will become the basis for establishing
goals and timetables.

Utilization analysis involves a three-step comparison of the
treatment of women and men with regard to recruitment, selection,
rank, salary, promotion, and conditions of employment. First, the
current distribution of women and men in each of these categories is
ascertained. If a college or university does not have current data on
the distribution of women and men by rank, sex, and department in
its central files, this information may be compiled at the department
level and then computed for the college or the institution as a whole.

The second step involves ascertaining underutilization—whether
the number and percentage of women in each category is smaller than

would be reasonably expected from their availability. Determining availability or the "available pool" (and therefore what a reasonable percentage of women would be) raises complex questions. Currently there are no uniform standards for determining the available pool, but it may be useful to review several standards that are now being employed. Most are based on national data, since it is assumed that academic recruitment is conducted on a national market.

One standard for determining the "available pool" of women for faculty positions is the percentage of women holding doctorates in a particular field. Thus, for example, if women hold 17 percent of all doctorates in sociology, the expected percentage of women on the faculty of a sociology department would be 17 percent. This same percentage should hold for women at each professorial rank.

A second and more refined standard for estimating the available pool of women faculty takes into account differences in the proportion of doctorates granted to women over time. Thus, the percentage of women full professors in a field might be expected to be low if the percentage of women doctorates was low a decade ago. If the percentage of women doctorates in that field is rising, we would expect a higher percentage of women at the assistant professor rank than among the tenured faculty.

It is recognized that institutions vary in the pools from which they draw new faculty members. In some cases the pool is national, while in others colleges and universities hire from a limited group of "feeder" graduate schools. If the proportion of women in the feeder schools is higher than the national figures, current expectations are that the contractors will use the feeder school figures in determining availability of women, while if the feeder schools graduate fewer women than the national average, contractors will use the national figures.

Other factors that should be considered in estimating an available pool, as listed in the OFCC regulations, include the number of women holding doctorates in the geographic area, the number of women applicants, the greatly expanding number of women graduate students who soon could fill the positions, and the number of women within the institution who could be promoted or transferred. In the past many qualified women with doctorates have been relegated to marginal research positions or one-year renewable lectureships for most of their academic careers. As faculty wives or local residents who have found themselves in a restricted local job market, some other women have settled for marginal employment. In addition, antinepotism regulations have often operated to deny or restrict the full employment of faculty wives. Women in each of these circumstances constitute a readily available and qualified source of faculty recruitment, and should be included in the estimates of the available pool.

It may also be useful to review standards for computing the available pool that have not been allowed by HEW compliance reviewers. The HEW compliance staff has not allowed departments to use different standards for women and men in estimating available pools of those with doctorates. For example, a department cannot calculate the available pool of women for faculty positions by taking the number of women holding doctorates, subtracting those who were not employed in academe, and then using this reduced number of women to calculate the proportion of women in the available pool unless it also "corrects" the available pool of men faculty in the same manner.

In general, when a department uses a method of calculating the available pool that results in a percentage of women that is lower than the time-corrected overall percentage of women holding doctorates in a field, there is a stronger burden of proof placed on the department to justify the standards used. Thus, if a department asserts that it recruits its faculty exclusively from the top five graduate departments in the country, and therefore estimated a much smaller pool of women than one based on all doctorates awarded nationally, it would have to submit data that established that each of its faculty was actually recruited from one of those five schools. OFCC regulations specifically state: "Women cannot be expected to possess higher qualifications than those of the lowest qualified incumbent."[4]

An additional objection has been raised to the standard of "top five departments" in computing the available pool. Just as many blacks were, and still are, excluded from elite educational institutions, women's exclusion from top institutions is perpetuated when it becomes the basis of estimates of employment pools. The same double-bind is created when professional schools recruit faculty from a pool of eligibles with certain types of professional experience. For example, the pool for faculty members at Yale Law School consists predominantly of persons who have clerked on the Supreme Court of the United States. Since only one woman has done so, continued application of this criterion could effectively exclude women from the available pool.

There has been no definitive ruling by either HEW or OFCC on the permissible standards for computing the available doctorate pool for faculty positions. However, compliance investigators have subjected exclusionary standards to strict scrutiny, and in several cases a department has been asked to broaden its basis for estimating the available pool.

Once a department or college has computed the available pool and estimated its underutilization of women, it comes to the third step in the utilization analysis: an examination of causes for underutilization and the development of affirmative action programs to correct them. First, a department must consider whether its sources and methods of recruitment give advantages to male candidates. Second, selection criteria and selection decisions must be examined. Third, rank and salary determinants, and the extent to which they may operate to the disadvantage of women, should be examined. For example, pay scales may be properly assigned by rank, yet women may be prevented by unfair requirements from moving up in rank.

The HEW Higher Education Guidelines note that women have sometimes been classified in "research associate" or "lecturer" ranks, from which promotion is rare, while men with the same qualifications are appointed to regular faculty positions and, therefore, have more opportunity to rise on the academic ladder.[5] Fourth, the standards for promotion and the application of those standards should be evaluated for possible sex bias. Finally, differences in conditions of employment, such as teaching load, research assistance, or leave privileges, should be examined.

Each of these areas requires review on both a departmental level and on a college or university level, since the causes for underutilization may not be restricted to, or initiated by, a single department.

Establishing Goals and Timetables

Under OFCC Regulations, §60-2.12 and HEW Guidelines, pp. 3-4, the next component of an affirmative action program is the establishment of specific goals and timetables to eliminate the deficiencies found in the utilization analysis.

Goals are numerical targets established to eliminate a demonstrated unequal utilization of women and men faculty, and to increase the proportional representation of women. Goals for eliminating inequities among presently employed women and men are easy to set, since the standard of parity required by HEW is clear. It is more difficult, however, to set reasonable goals to increase the representation of women on the faculty because of the complexities in establishing standards of fair representation. Roughly the same guidelines suggested in estimating the available pool for the utilization analysis should be used in establishing appropriate goals.

Goals should be established both by the department and by the college or university in each of the five areas covered in the utilization analysis: recruitment, selection, salary and rank equity, promotion, and conditions of employment. In some areas, such as recruitment, the university-wide goals will merely summarize the goals set by individual departments. But in other areas university goals may involve new programs that cannot be handled on the departmental level. For example, the goal of eliminating all salary inequities or the goal of establishing part-time tenure positions would prob-

ably have to be implemented through university-wide policies and procedures. Even in setting departmental goals, there must be some
consultation and coordination with deans and affirmative action officials because departmental goals must take into account budgetary
conditions, anticipated turnover, and the creation of new faculty positions.

Goals must be linked to specific target dates for their attainment.
OFCC usually requires that they be specified for a one-year period,
although these yearly goals are expected to be part of a more comprehensive three-to-five-year plan. Goals that are set too far in the
future, without yearly plans, indicate the lack of a serious commitment to affirmative action.

In addition to requiring goals of both schools and departments,
OFCC regulations require that all goals be specified by rank (for
instance, a goal of hiring 10 female full professors). They should be
stated in numerical terms as well as in percentages, or departments
may discover that they have committed themselves to hiring a fraction of a person.

When deficiencies exist, departments are required to establish
separate goals for minorities and women and to break down the goals
for each minority group by sex. When this is done, a department
cannot count a minority female twice (as is typically done with black
women) and thereby circumvent the purpose of the compliance program.

A Program of Action to Attain
Established Goals

Perhaps the most important component of an affirmative action
program consists of the concrete steps to achieve specified goals
(OFCC Regulations $60-2.24, and HEW Guidelines, pp. 4-14). We
shall confine our discussion here to a brief review of the types of
program enumerated by OFCC and HEW; detailed suggestions and
references to existing programs will be discussed later.

Action programs should be established for each problem area:
recruitment procedures, selection criteria, salary equity, promotion procedures, and improved conditions of employment.

Programs for recruitment include contacting women's organizations that are prepared to refer women with specific skills; including
women in all phases of the recruitment process; active recruiting efforts at schools with large numbers of women students; and specific
mention of women in recruitment letters, brochures, and job listings.

With regard to the selection process, OFCC regulations require
the careful examination of selection criteria to "insure that the require

ments in themselves do not constitute inadvertent discrimination."[6]
Other guidelines include elimination of requirements that screen out
a disproportionate number of women; an explicit statement of standards
for selection and promotion; the elimination of such irrelevant selection criteria as marital status, dependency status, or responsibility
for minor children; and training of all personnel involved in the selection process to insure elimination of bias in the decisions.

OFCC's regulations for insuring equal opportunity for promotion
include periodic review and evaluation of all female employees; review of employment criteria to insure that women are not required to
possess higher qualifications than those of the lowest qualified incumbent; a written justification from department chairpersons when apparently qualified women are passed over for promotions; and the open
listing or announcement of all promotional opportunities.

Finally, with regard to establishing conditions of benefit to employees, OFCC guidelines suggest offering child-care facilities,
housing, and transportation programs where needed. OFCC requires
that social and recreational activities be open to both sexes.

Establishing Internal Audit and
Reporting Systems

According to OFCC Regulations, §60-2.25, and HEW Guidelines,
p. 16, responsibility for establishing a means of monitoring all
phases of the affirmative action program lies with the affirmative action official. Order no. 4 requires that periodic written progress
reports be submitted to the official by department chairpersons and
deans. These reports should include the department's utilization analysis, goals and timetables, and an evaluation of the progress of its
action programs.

In order for the monitoring procedure to work effectively, departmental reports should be submitted semiannually. This allows
for a midyear check on departmental personnel decisions and for intervention, when necessary, to forestall a discriminatory decision.
An alternative to semiannual reports would be to require the signa-
ture of the affirmative action official on all departmental requests
for appointment, tenure, promotion, termination, salary increase,
or the denial of any of these. By withholding approval, an affirmative
action official may question and delay any recommendation that seems
to violate a department's goals.

In general, academic departments have been reluctant to allow
administrative review of their personnel decisions, for fear of interference with important academic freedoms, even though affirmative
action officials and assisting committee members typically are drawn

from faculty ranks. It is important to note, however, that academic
freedom has never meant freedom to deny a qualified person a job
or advancement on the basis of race or sex. When personal and subjective judgments enter decisions concerning employment, the review
processes suggested by OFCC and HEW simply insure that such judgments do not violate the faculty's own goals for hiring on the basis of
merit.

Support for Other Action Programs, with Special
Attention to Increasing the Future
Position of Women in Academe

OFFCC Regulations, §60-2.13 i, j, and §60-2,26, state that educational institutions are obliged to encourage and train women for
faculty positions and to expand the opportunities available to women
in academe. Although most programs would focus on graduate students, guidance and counseling programs are appropriate for undergraduate women as well. Other procedures to encourage the participation of women students, especially of older women students, might
include the abolition of sex-based admissions quotas, the loosening
of regulations concerning part-time study, abolition of age or marital
restrictions on financial aid, and other efforts to insure the equal
training and support of women students at all levels.

STRUCTURAL PITFALLS

Ineffective programs seem to suffer from one of three difficulties:
the affirmative action official was not given sufficient rank and power;
a nonacademic person was appointed to the position; or the affirmative
action official lacked a commitment to improving the status of women.

With regard to rank, we recommend that the affirmative action
official be given a rank equivalent to that of a provost or vice-president. In a large university each college or school might appoint an
affirmative action dean to work with the university-wide affirmative
action provost and to take direct responsibility for routine supervision
of the program within a school or college.

The second difficulty has been caused by the appointment of a single affirmative action official with responsibility for both academic
and nonacademic employees. A person trained in industrial "job analysis" does not have the experience or the knowledge to handle the
problems of academic personnel. Because of the strong tradition of
faculty autonomy, department chairpersons are likely to resent "directives" from someone who has little understanding of academic cri-

teria and standards of professional competence. Similarly, a university professor usually has not had sufficient experience in dealing with nonacademic job classifications for competent supervision of the nonacademic employee compliance plan. For these reasons it seems advisable to appoint different officers to deal with academic and nonacademic personnel.

A third common reason for the failure in the university affirmative action office has been the appointment of individuals who are not sympathetic to or knowledgeable about the problems confronting academic women. To date a majority of institutions have appointed black males to supervise affirmative action programs; understandably, these men have often been more absorbed with minority concerns than with the problems of academic women. Again, it seems wise to have two separate programs, one for minorities and one for women, to prevent conflicts of interest and charges of favoritism within the program. Although the presence of two programs may double the pressure on academic departments with respect to achieving affirmative action goals, it may backfire and result in competition between the two programs. It is absolutely essential that the two programs work together and try to reinforce each other.

Ideally, a person who is committed to improving the status of academic women should be appointed to the position of affirmative action provost for women. This person must, however, be equally concerned with minority women and make sure that they are not doubly victimized. To date minority women have often been excluded from programs for both women and minorities because programs for women have concentrated on white women, while programs for minorities have concentrated on black or Chicano men. The University of Vermont has faced this problem by appointing a black woman to direct the affirmative action program for the entire university.

In recommending that different persons be appointed to deal with women, minorities, and academic and nonacademic employees, it might seem that we have restricted our recommendations to large universities. In fact, a school like Michigan State University is able to support an affirmative action staff of nine persons. However, we have not ignored the personnel limitations of small colleges. Affirmative action officials may have other administrative responsibilities in addition to affirmative action. Our recommendation is that different personnel of high rank be responsible for each group. In a small college these positions easily might be filled by college deans or by faculty members working half-time on affirmative action.

Because of the power and responsibility concentrated in the office of an affirmative action provost, several universities have established advisory committees to work with the officer in directing the affirmative action program. These committees include faculty with expertise in statistics, data processing, and law, as well as significant representation from faculty and staff women, department chairpersons, and administrative personnel. In one university the advisory committee sent out guidelines to assist departments in establishing appropriate goals. In another it divided itself into smaller groups to meet with recalcitrant department chairpersons, and in a third it issued directives for equalizing salaries. Whether the advisory committee takes an active role in program implementation, or defines itself as a committee to review the programs implemented by the affirmative action officer, it can provide an important service in facilitating affirmative action progress.

While an affirmative action program without an effective structure is less likely to succeed, structure alone cannot guarantee success. It is most important to emphasize the necessity of having people who are deeply committed to affirmative action goals involved in every stage of the process. Real implementation of an action program is assured only when those who are committed to it are allowed to play a crucial role.

SPECIFIC ACTION PROGRAMS

In this section we will suggest a range of possible action programs, drawing on many that have already been instituted in colleges and universities. Our aim is to assist those who are committed to affirmative action in devising the most effective methods of achieving equality for women and men in higher education. The legal requirements we have enumerated may be viewed as a creative challenge to each educational community to design an action program that is both effective and uniquely suited to it.

It is impossible to recommend foolproof procedures for achieving affirmative action goals. Although any one of the following programs may be viewed as difficult, awkward, inconvenient, or too timid, it is hoped that some of them will be useful as they are, or that they will suggest modifications more suitable to particular institutions.

Recruitment Programs

Because women frequently are excluded from traditional recruitment networks, departments seeking women faculty probably will want to try new recruitment techniques that are designed specifically to locate women candidates. Therefore, on the departmental level, we recommend the following:

1. All recruitment communications should state that a department is actively seeking qualified women candidates.

2. Contact professional women's organizations to request the referral of qualified candidates. Most professional organizations have women's caucuses or commissions; a list of these may be obtained from Ruth Oltman of the American Association of University Women, Washington, D.C.

3. List positions and job openings in professional journals. For example, open listing is currently the university-wide policy at the University of Minnesota.

4. List positions and job openings in women's journals and through women's organizations. Women's journals, including Spokeswoman, KNOW news service, Women Today, and Ms. will announce job openings; and such women's organizations as the National Organization for Women and the Talent Bank of the Business and Professional Women's Organization will refer qualified women upon request.

5. Involve women in all phases of the recruitment process. This involvement includes both membership on departmental recruitment committees and recruitment at professional meetings. If a department does not have a woman on its faculty, it might ask a woman faculty member in a related discipline or a woman graduate student to serve on its recruitment committee.

6. Consult professional rosters and national directories of association memberships, which list members (both women and men) by area of specialty and provide information on awards and research interests. Some professional organizations (for example, the American Sociological Association) publish a list of all prospective doctoral candidates every year, with pertinent information on each.

7. Consult regional and national rosters and referral services for academic women. In contrast with the above sources, which list both women and men in academe, special referral services and directories have been established for academic women. The Higher Education Resource Center at Brown University and the American Association for the Advancement of Science are developing national rosters of academic women.

8. Consult national and regional associations of black and Chicano professionals. Efforts to locate minority women can be assisted by such organizations as the National Council of Negro Women, the National Chicana Foundation, and black women's sororities and service groups (such as Delta Sigma Theta, Alpha Kappa Alpha, and Zeta Phi Beta). Conferences such as the annual conference of black professionals in higher education might also be helpful. Similar referral organizations should be consulted for Asian women, native American women, and Puerto Rican women.

9. Solicit qualified applicants from schools that have large female student populations, such as women's schools and schools in metropolitan areas. For minority women, the alumnae offices of schools like Spelman College in Atlanta should be contacted, as well as schools in the urban North.

10. Invite the consultation of prominent women scholars.

11. Consider women who have held marginal positions in the department for promotion to regular faculty appointments. Women who hold the title of lecturer, instructor, or research associate should be considered for ladder positions. Michigan State University, and the Universities of Pittsburgh, Michigan, and Washington, have specified that departments must consider "marginal" women for regular appointments. Duke University goes even further, and states that if two professionals are equally qualified, the marginal person should be given priority in hiring.

12. Consider professional women working in independent research institutions, in government agencies, in private industry, or foundations for faculty appointments.

13. Consider hiring those who have received their doctorates from the department. Although many departments have informal rules against in-hiring, this may be an appropriate time to reconsider such regulations because they deprive many departments of a good source of new "woman power." If a department has certified a significant number of women as worthy professionals by granting them doctorates, they may be worthy of consideration for a faculty position at the same university.

14. Consider unsolicited applications. Although many departments have traditionally ignored unsolicited applications, one indication of good-faith efforts is a willingness to consider applications from all women, whatever their source.

15. Consider tandem teams. Husbands and wives have typically had great difficulty in finding employment in the same university because of antinepotism regulations. Good-faith efforts might be indicated by a department's willingness to encourage academic couples and to consider them for employment.

There is some concern among women's groups that departments will merely go through the motions of using the above procedures but continue to hire persons recommended through informal networks. One check is provided by OFCC regulations requiring that departments maintain applicant flow data (the source of referral and the review procedures for each of the candidates considered) and applicant rejection ratios by sex. These data should be monitored by women within the department to insure that they are not "created" after the fact. Such records may prove useful to the department for its own

affirmative action analyses, as well as for documentation of good-
faith efforts.

One successful recruitment program was organized by Sheila
Tobias, associate provost at Wesleyan University, who has a general
fund to bring women scholars to the campus as lecturers. Since all
departments are required to submit their recruitment priorities to
the provost's office, Tobias can coordinate these lecturers with recruitment efforts of departments. In this way a department has an opportunity to review potential candidates with no financial drain on department budgets, and students benefit greatly from the presence of
visiting women scholars. Other university-wide programs, such as
the one instituted at the California Institute of Technology, include
workshops for faculty involved in recruiting. These programs present techniques to increase the representation of women on the faculty
and encourage commitment to affirmative action hiring.

One of the most effective university-wide programs to encourage
the recruitment of women faculty is the provision of special university
funds to be used for their hiring. The potential impact of this kind
of stimulus is illustrated by the recent experience of the University
of California at Davis. A few years ago the chancellor and the vice-
chancellor for academic affairs sent a number of appeals to department chairmen encouraging the recruitment of minority faculty.
When departmental recommendations for new faculty appointments
were reviewed, however, most chairmen contended that they had not
been able to locate qualified minority faculty. The following year the
chancellor established special funds for hiring minority faculty;
these funds allowed departments to gain a new ladder position if they
hired a minority scholar. Within a year departments that had previously been unable to locate "qualified" minority persons found an
abundance of outstanding black and Chicano scholars whom they wanted
to hire and were vying for the special positions.

Efforts to retain women who are already on the faculty are as important as recruitment to improve the overall proportion of women
faculty. The authors of the affirmative action plan at the University
of Pittsburgh have noted that crucial factors in attracting new women
to the faculty are the current atmosphere and the support given to
women already on the faculty.

                      Programs for the Selection Process

Neither the criteria for faculty hiring nor the procedures for applying these criteria should give an advantage on the basis of sex.
However, applying egalitarian criteria is difficult even when no bias
is intended. Departments traditionally have relied upon the judgments

of friends to assess the merits of candidates for junior faculty positions. These judgments often are affected by unconscious stereotypes about the interest and competence of women—women are less committed to intellectual careers, women are less able to deal with "high-level theory," and so on. Because of the crucial role that such consciously or unconsciously biased assessments have played in the past, the increased pressures on departments to justify their hiring decisions (by making their selection criteria and procedures explicit) probably will have the positive effect of pushing all departments to develop more effective and sex-neutral means of evaluating a candidate's potential.

Given the wide variety of departments wishing to develop affirmative action programs, it is impossible to devise a set of uniform criteria and procedures that will fit the needs of every department. Thus, some of the following suggestions may not be applicable to certain departments, and others may have to be altered or changed to be effective. In the selection of faculty we recommend the following:

1. Departments should specify their selection criteria for all faculty appointments. It is important that selection criteria be specified before individual candidates are considered; this will insure that ad hoc criteria are not being invoked to justify the selection of male candidates. Moreover, the relative weight given to letters of recommendation, teaching experience, area of specialization, graduate training, publications, and other factors should be established. The HEW Guidelines state: "An employer must establish in reasonable detail, and make available upon request, the standards and procedures which govern all employment practices . . . including the criteria by which qualifications for appointment, retention, or promotion are judged."[7]

2. Departments should examine their selection criteria to insure that they are not sex-biased. Seemingly neutral standards may in fact eliminate prospective female candidates. For example, rigorous restrictions with regard to the prestige of the doctorate-granting institution or department, the amount of research support received, or expertise in some specialty area may exclude members of one sex more than the other. Because women have been systematically barred from entering some institutions, they should not be required to hold a degree from such institutions. Neither should women be rejected because of smaller records of research support, since they have had less access to research funds in the past.

3. Departments may not raise or change hiring criteria when considering women candidates. OFCC regulations specifically state that women should not be required to possess higher qualifications than those of the lowest qualified incumbent.[8] For example, if a psy-

chology department hired a male assistant professor in 1972 who had
not published, it cannot decide that each new female assistant professor in 1973 must have a published book.

4. Departments must insure that women are not assigned a lower
rank in hiring decisions. The HEW Guidelines state: "In many institutions women are more often assigned initially to lower academic
ranks than are men. A study by one disciplinary association showed
that women tend to be offered a first appointment at the rank of Instructor rather than the rank of Assistant Professor three times more
often than men with identical qualifications."[9] Where there is no valid
basis for such differential treatment such a practice is in violation of
the Executive Order.[10]

5. Departments should insure that the academic work and recommendations of women candidates are processed in the same manner as
those of men candidates. The review process for candidates under
serious consideration, including an examination of their written work,
letters of recommendation, teaching experience, and a personal inter-
view, should be identical for persons of each sex. To insure impartial consideration, some schools have instituted a system of blind
reading of the candidates' written work. Another way of insuring an
objective review might be to submit vita and written work to outside
consultants for a second reading and evaluation.

6. Departments should insure that irrelevant considerations,
such as marital status and the presence of dependent children, are
not part of the evaluation of a woman candidate. Consideration of
marriage and parenthood are specifically forbidden by OFCC regulations. Even if such considerations are not raised directly, a woman's
"commitment" or availability to students is often questioned. In
some situations it is assumed that family considerations would prevent a woman from moving, and she is automatically excluded from
serious consideration. Departments should consider all women "available" for new opportunities unless they have been informed otherwise
by her. Other irrelevant social characteristics may intrude into a
department's evaluations of women. Because members of the same
academic department often become friends, women candidates may be
viewed as less suitable to become "one of the boys." Such irrelevant
considerations as family background, athletic ability, congeniality,
and political preferences have been used to exclude other minorities
in the past; they should be eliminated in considering the academic
competence of all candidates, including women.

7. Departments should afford women candidates the opportunity
to present themselves and their work on recruitment visits. An important indicator of good-faith efforts is the number of women who
have been invited to the campus for a recruitment visit. Equally important is the way in which they are treated on these visits. For ex-

ample, one department did not schedule colloquiums for its women candidates because they allegedly did not want to put too much pressure on them. The result was that members of the department saw the women candidates only socially, and received the impression that they were less serious and less intellectually oriented than the men candidates.

8. Women should be involved in all stages of the selection process: establishing criteria; evaluating vitae, written work, and letters of recommendation; and reviewing the relative merits of the candidates. By involving women in the selection process, a department may be better able to avoid the unconscious bias that often enters into judgments of merit.

In addition to these procedures for insuring equal opportunities for women in departmental selection processes, some selection policies—such as antinepotism regulations—require revision on the college or university level. The HEW Guidelines explicitly prohibit antinepotism policies:

> Policies or practices which prohibit or limit the simultaneous employment of two members of the same family and which have an adverse impact upon one sex or the other are in violation of the Executive Order. . . . Antinepotism regulations in most cases operate to deny employment opportunity to a wife rather than a husband.
> . . . If an individual has been denied opportunity for employment, advancement or benefits on the basis of an anti-nepotism rule or practice, that action is discriminatory and prohibited under the Executive Order.[11]

However, although antinepotism policies are prohibited, HEW does allow "reasonable restriction" on an individual's participation in decisions involving a member of his or her family.[12] The American Association of University Professors' policy on faculty appointment and family relationship is cited as an example of a reasonable restriction on limiting family members from participating in institutional decisions involving a direct benefit (initial appointment, retention, promotion, salary) to members of their immediate family.[13]

The positive effect of removing antinepotism regulations is illustrated by recent events at the University of Washington. When the nepotism rule was changed, a review was made of the status of women who held positions in the same departments as their husbands. It resulted in a number of qualified women being recommended for promotion at various academic levels. The University of Washington is currently reviewing women who hold positions outside their husbands' departments, and is committed to make similar adjustments in appointments wherever women have been given lower level or off-ladder positions because of the old nepotism rule.

Programs to Achieve Salary Equity

Programs for achieving salary equity have two primary aims: the elimination of salary differences between women and men faculty of equal rank, experience, and contribution; and the awarding of back pay to women who have received lower salaries than men as a result of past discrimination. It has often been assumed that salary equity for women and men will result in the complete standardization of salary among faculty of the same rank; this is not so. Departments and universities will continue to determine the criteria for salary distinctions, but institutions are likely to vary in the relative emphasis placed on such criteria as good teaching, original research, service to the community, or straight seniority. Whatever the standards for salary distinctions, they should be clearly stated and applied equally to men and women. Salary equity with regard to sex precludes only salary distinctions made solely on the basis of sex; it does not preclude other distinctions deemed significant by a faculty.

Specific programs to achieve salary equity have been established in many schools; but differences in size, financial resources, and the degree of past discrimination have resulted in many different types of program. In some institutions, such as the University of Wisconsin and the University of Southern Florida, equalization was done on a department level. At these universities, if the salaries of female faculty members were below those of males of the same rank and experience within their department, women's salaries were raised accordingly. In contrast, at other schools (and more typically smaller schools) salary comparisons have been conducted on a college or university level. A combination of the two approaches was used at the University of Maine. In the first phase of the Maine program, minimum salaries were established for all ranks; and salaries falling below the rank minimum were raised to those levels. In the second phase, inequities between men and women faculty of the same rank within departments were equalized.

Some institutions have established programs to equalize salaries between departments when women faculty were found to be concentrated in departments or schools with lower overall pay scales. For example, the University of Minnesota allocated $84,500 for upgrading salaries in the School of Nursing, the School of Home Economics, and the Office of Student Affairs. Other institutions with seemingly effective written programs for achieving salary equity include Stanford University, the California Institute of Technology, the Universities of Michigan, Oregon, and Massachusetts, and Michigan State University.

With regard to the second component of achieving salary equity—
that of awarding back pay—educational institutions have been much
slower to devise programs in accord with the law. Back pay is mone-
tary award equal to the difference between the salary a woman actually
received and the amount she would have received if she had not been
the victim of sex-based salary discrimination.

The legal precedents for awarding compensation to victims of
salary discrimination in industry have been clearly established under
the Equal Pay Act of 1963. Unfortunately, academic women were not
covered by this strong legislation (and the equally strong compliance
staff of the Wage and Hour Division of the Department of Labor) until
March 1972. But academic women who have been the victims of salary discrimination after March 1972 can now be assured of court-or-
dered back pay awards under the Equal Pay Act (and under Title VII
of the Civil Rights Act, which also began to cover academic women in
March 1972 by virtue of the 1972 educational amendments). Women
seeking back pay for salary discrimination prior to 1972 fall under
the jurisdiction of HEW. According to HEW's most recent guidelines,
it supports the principles of back pay[14] and has already ordered back-
pay awards for women faculty at several universities, most notably
at the University of Michigan.

Programs to Achieve Equity in
Rank and Promotion

Salary and rank are closely linked. Inequities in salary alone
are often miniscule in comparison with salary inequities that result
from inequities in rank and promotion. As Helen Astin and Alan Bayer
have demonstrated, women have been required to have higher qualifications for promotion than men and typically have remained at each
faculty rank longer than their male colleagues.[15] To correct this
situation, procedures should be established to review the rank of all
women faculty and to recommend promotions of those who have been
victims of rank inequity. In addition, all future decisions concerning
rank and promotion should be handled in a way to insure the elimination of sex-discriminatory processes.

In reviewing the rank distribution of current faculty and the departmental standards and procedures for promotion, the following
points should be covered:

1. A department should state its standards for promotion to each
faculty rank by specifying the relative weight it will give to teaching,
publication, research, service, administration, and length of service.
Criteria for tenure also should be specified.

2. The rank of each woman faculty member should be reviewed. Rank equity may be evaluated in two ways. First, one can compare the rank of women and men of the same "academic age" within a department—that is, those who received their doctorates in the same year. In departments too small for this comparison, it is more useful to examine promotion rates by computing the average number of years that women and men have spent in each professional rank. By this method the promotion rate of a female faculty member would be compared with the average promotion rate for male faculty in the same department.

3. If a department feels that a lower rank for a woman is justified, it should submit a written report stating its reasons. Acceptable reasons for a rank discrepancy should be based on the departmental standards, and might include an absence from professional work or a lack of comparable scholarly productivity.

4. When a department submits justification for rank differences between women and men, it might include an analysis of the causes of the differences and, where appropriate, an action program for eliminating the causes. For example, if a department has given a woman a heavier teaching load or less research assistance in the past, then compensatory steps (such as increased research assistance) may be taken as part of the department's action program.

Programs to Achieve Equity in
Conditions of Employment

In the review of OFCC regulations, it was noted that the utilization analysis required of each department included a comparison of the conditions of employment for male and female faculty. Employment conditions include teaching load, research facilities, research and teaching assistance, office space, secretarial assistance, and teaching assignments. They also include the type of faculty appointment and the opportunities and procedures for promotion.

A review might begin with a comparison of teaching conditions of male and female faculty over the past few years, examining the relative number of courses taught, the size of the classes, the number of graduate seminars taught, the hours the classes met, and the amount of teaching assistance received for a class of a particular size. If differences by sex are found, affirmative action may be warranted. For example, HEW's review at the University of Massachusetts included suggestions for reducing the teaching load of several women faculty members to the average load for men faculty, or redistributing the teaching load in specific departments.

Departments should also consider conditions of employment with respect to research. They can compare the research assistants, facilities, equipment, computer time, and financial support that have been afforded women and men faculty. For example, the lack of comparable laboratory space and equipment for women faculty in the biological sciences was specifically noted in HEW's review of Rutgers University.

Responsibilities of faculty, such as serving on department committees, advising students, and supervising dissertations, also should be reviewed and divided equitably. Compensation for past misallocation of work may be appropriate.

In each of these areas, compensation should not be confused with reward. If a woman is compensated for past inequities by receiving a light teaching load, she should not then be saddled with advising because she has "more free time." Although inequities in employment conditions may be corrected on the departmental level, it is clear that some of the compensatory programs require university-level support. Action programs on the college or university level might include special research or teaching leaves (for those who have carried unusually heavy or undesirable teaching loads in the past) and special research support, as is now the policy for junior faculty at the University of California.

One of the most important university-wide programs for faculty women is the provision for part-time faculty appointments on the regular tenure ladder. A part-time faculty member normally would carry half of the regular teaching load, but would be considered a regular member of the department with full faculty privileges. She or he would serve on departmental committees, have a proportional share of departmental responsibilities and student advisees, and would receive prorated benefits (such as salary, medical coverage, retirement benefits, sabbatical leave). As first instituted at Princeton, part-time ladder faculty are allowed a proportionately longer period of time before review for tenure. Harvard, Princeton, Yale, Wisconsin, Stanford, and the University of California at Berkeley have established provisions for part-time ladder appointments. Several of these institutions have also revised their tenure rules so that part-time appointments may be particularly suited to the needs of parents (both male and female) with small children. Such positions provide the department with a broader range of faculty specialties and may serve to increase the range of courses a department can offer.

Programs to Achieve Equity in Fringe Benefits

Universities and colleges are required by law to provide women and men with equal employment benefits. Those that are directly related to work include sabbaticals, travel to professional meetings, faculty fellowships, summer salaries, and research grants. Since many of these benefits have already been reviewed, we simply reiterate that departments and schools should examine the distribution of benefits among women and men faculty, and take whatever steps are necessary to insure that they are awarded equitably.

Employment benefits that are not directly related to work include health and life insurance, retirement programs, and day care. With regard to the first two, it is legally required that the same type of coverage be offered to all employees. Further, it is required that maternity leaves be treated like any other temporary disability. Princeton and Stanford have extended faculty women's contracts and postponed tenure decisions one year for each year taken off for child-bearing and/or rearing, up to two years. These benefits could easily be extended to male faculty willing to assume equal responsibility for child rearing. The University of Maine has instituted a program of granting both women and men faculty leave for child-rearing purposes for periods up to two years. Retirement plans for women must also be equal to those for men in regard to the age at which one can retire, payment schedules, and support for a surviving spouse. Provision of day care services is legally optional, but it is suggested in both OFCC's order no. 4 and HEW's Guidelines.[16]

In addition to the fringe benefits reviewed, faculty may be provided with meals, housing, transportation, or recreational opportunities and facilities. Each institution should examine the full range of fringe benefits available to their faculty, to make sure that they contain no inequality. For example, HEW's report of findings to Brown University indicated that such fringe benefits as moving expenses for new faculty, and housing and maid service for administrators, were granted to men more often than to women staff members.

Programs to Achieve Equity in the
Training of Future Women Faculty

The most direct and profitable way a university can expend time and money to increase the number of women available for faculty positions is to insure the equal training of women graduate students. A full discussion of the situation of women graduate students is beyond the scope of this section, but a few examples of affirmative-action plans for graduate students suggest the direction they might take:

1. A college, university, or department should actively recruit female graduate students, as is now being done at Stanford Business School.

2. Age restrictions for admission to graduate school should be reconsidered, and the admission of older women who have taken time out for child rearing could be encouraged.

3. Special efforts can be made to locate, readmit, and assist financially those women who have completed everything but their dissertations.

4. All admissions quotas (such as those that have existed in medical and law schools) should be abolished, with students admitted on a merit basis only.

5. A university should ensure the elimination of sex bias in granting of fellowships, teaching or research assistantships, and other forms of financial aid awarded to graduate students. Age restrictions for these awards also should be abolished.

6. The university might provide for part-time study and part-time financial support for women and men with family responsibilities that preclude full-time study.

7. Departments should insure that there is no sex bias in the dissertation support and guidance given to women and men graduate students.

8. Departments might give more assistance to their women doctorate-holders in obtaining employment.

Other Programs to Achieve Equity
for Academic Women

The wide range of programs and activities within a university can have the cumulative effect of making faculty women feel either very welcome or totally excluded from the university community. We offer the following suggestions for improving the overall position of women in the academic community:

1. Assure representation of women in crucial decision-making positions throughout the university. In addition to assuming the representation of women at all levels of the university administration, the provost might appoint a special committee to review the representation of women in decision-making positions throughout the university—on the Board of Trustees, the Budget Committee, the Educational Policy Committee, and so on.

2. Provide support for women's programs and activities, such as a women's center, lectures by academic and professional women, a film series on women, women's athletic programs, guidance and career counseling, a women's newsletter. The affirmative action provost might further review the representation of women throughout the university community by considering the recognition accorded wo-

men as commencement speakers, as recipients of honorary degrees
at commencement, as invited public university lecturers, and as the
president's or dean's representative at outside functions.

3. Establishment of a women's studies program and the institution of courses and research on women. Both women faculty and students should be afforded the opportunity to study their own history,
biology, psychology, sociology, art, and literature. The existence
of courses and seminars on women will provide added stimulus to
faculty research in these areas and may provide both women and men
faculty with new analytic tools.

4. An ombudsman for women. The duties of an ombudsman usually are flexible, and the person is empowered to provide assistance
in resolving individual complaints of sex discrimination and in matters
such as health insurance, arranging a sabbatical, or obtaining research facilities.

Action Programs to Insure Faculty Members a
Means of Appealing Department Decisions

An essential component of any action program is the establishment of internal grievance procedures. Such procedures should provide for an impartial review of individual complaints of sex discrimination, as well as for a review of general complaints about the implementation of the affirmative-action program. Procedures should be
adequate to deal with complaints about recruitment, selection, hiring,
salary, rank, promotion, tenure, and termination decisions, and
should be widely publicized. The University of Hawaii and Michigan
State University have developed excellent internal grievance procedures.

Programs for Reviewing and Sanctioning
Affirmative Action Progress

As noted earlier, OFCC requires that departments submit periodic reports of their progress in meeting affirmative action goals.
In addition, departments may have to demonstrate "good-faith efforts"
by providing documentation to show that they followed the procedures
outlined in their action program.

Two means of reviewing departmental progress have been suggested: semiannual departmental reports, to allow a review of intended personnel decisions before they are approved; and provisions
for the review of all departmental personnel decisions, at the time
they are recommended, before a department can make an offer of an

appointment. Such a review might be conducted by the affirmative action provost, the affirmative action dean of the college, or a special faculty committee with adequate representation of women. This type of review of all personnel decisions is now required at Columbia University, Brown University, and the University of California at Berkeley.

A review of departmental decisions and progress is an essential part of any action program. It serves to demonstrate good-faith efforts on the part of the university in monitoring the effectiveness of its program. In addition, it allows the administration to sanction compliance and noncompliance with the affirmative action goals. Compliance does not depend on attaining the goals of an affirmative action program, but rests on documented evidence of good-faith efforts. Here we wish to suggest how universities might cope with departments that neither achieve their affirmative action goals nor document that they made good-faith efforts to do so.

The first step in dealing with such a department would focus on negotiation and persuasion, through special meetings with the chairperson and faculty, to assist them in improving their action program and strengthening their commitment to affirmative action goals. The OFCC regulations do not specify what steps might be taken if negotiation and persuasion do not work; they only state that other recommendations should be provided. This is of critical importance, however, since without concrete sanctions to enforce an affirmative action program, the plan becomes a series of hollow promises. Good faith efforts on the part of a college or university mean that the institution will do everything possible to insure compliance with its action program.

To insure compliance with affirmative action goals, a school might consider the following positive and negative sanctions:

1. Publicizing departmental success or failure in meeting goals through periodic reports in the campus newspaper or alumni bulletin.

2. Providing special funds to departments for affirmative action hiring.

3. Rewarding departments by allowing them to retain the ladder positions given to them for affirmative action hiring. (However, if a position is not continuously filled by affirmative action hiring, it might revert back to the affirmative action provost for allocation to another department.)

4. Linking increases and decreases in departmental operating budgets to progress in meeting affirmative action goals.

5. Linking all faculty appointments to affirmative action progress.

6. Instituting a strict review of all departmental decisions in problem departments. At the University of Minnesota, if a unit of the

university fails to correct existing inequities in regard to women and is unable to demonstrate that the reasons for failure are beyond its control, all of its personnel decisions become subject to college-level or central administrative review until the unit appears capable of eliminating discrimination by itself.

7. Linking university travel funds to affirmative action progress. Travel allowances for members of departments that have not met affirmative action goals might be limited (with the exception of travel for recruitment purposes.)

8. Linking salary and merit increases to affirmative action progress, whereby salary increases or merit increases might not be granted in departments that have not met affirmative action goals (especially those for salary equity).

9. Linking budget decisions on the expansion and contraction of departments to affirmative action progress.

10. Linking university research grants to departments' affirmative action progress.

11. Linking university approval of outside grant applications to affirmative action progress.

12. The affirmative action provost could recommend that an uncooperative department chairperson be replaced by a new one more sympathetic to affirmative action.

The extent to which individual faculty members of a department should be penalized for the failure of a department as a whole to meet affirmative action goals is a difficult issue. However, we believe that all departmental faculty should share the responsibility for affirmative action. By instituting individual as well as collective sanctions for the goals, the chances of insuring commitment of all faculty are maximized. Further, it is important to structure the situation so that both individuals and departments are rewarded for meeting affirmative action goals and so that those who remain in opposition to the goals will lose their power in a department or be ostracized by their colleagues. This kind of structure contrasts sharply with the current situation in most departments, in which a faculty minority can greatly retard and hamper a majority committed to affirmative action. Because academic decisions often require a consensus for new faculty hiring (or, in many cases, give all senior faculty veto power), a recalcitrant minority may make affirmative action hiring impossible. Only when those who are opposed to affirmative action are penalized will discriminatory practices cease to exist. Without sanctions, affirmative action plans remain "paper tigers"; with sanctions, they are turned into forceful directives for necessary social change.

THE PROBLEMS OF IMPLEMENTATION
AND UNCONSCIOUS BIAS

Although we have devoted a great amount of attention to specific suggestions for writing an affirmative action plan, it is obvious that even the best plan can be ineffective if those charged with its execution are not fully committed to its implementation. While an effective written plan provides the necessary preconditions for a successful program, it alone cannot guarantee success; equally important are all those individuals who must implement the affirmative action procedures, from the affirmative action provost to the individual faculty member involved in departmental hiring and promotion decisions.

Strong plans that have become "paper tigers" seem to have suffered from one of the following problems: those responsible for implementation were not sufficiently committed to affirmative action goals to insure adherence to the plan; those responsible for implementation were not aware of the ways in which their unconscious biases served to undermine the program; or the weight of the institutional structure undermined those committed to affirmative action changes. There is not much advice we can offer on how to deal with the first problem—that of lack of commitment. We have already suggested that affirmative action officials be chosen on the basis of their commitment to the program, and that feminists be actively involved in implementing every part of the affirmative action program. In the next section we shall add some suggestions to assist women in counteracting ineffective administrations. In this section we focus on the problems of unconscious bias and on overcoming established institutional patterns.

Some of those involved in implementing affirmative action programs may retain an unconscious bias against the full participation of women in academia. Most of these persons (and they do include women) have good intentions and are rarely aware of either their bias or its effects. The following are several ways in which unconscious bias operates.

First, although review committees may read the academic work of both male and female candidates, they may not realize that they are evaluating the work differently. For example, a friend of the author's noted that on one department recruitment committee, when articles had been coauthored by a male and a female, the committee assumed that the male was the senior author of the paper. When questioned, two explanations were that the male's name appeared first and that if the woman's name appeared first, it began with an earlier letter of the alphabet, which implied alphabetical criteria for listing, or the male was being courteous in allowing her name to ap-

pear first. While norms for which author's name shall appear first
vary by field, and it is therefore difficult to suggest standardized
rules for dealing with coauthored work, it is important to be aware of
unconscious assumptions about women's contributions—and to guard
against denying them credit for their scholarly achievements.

A more subtle form of unconscious bias affects the evaluation of
a scholarly article. In an experimental evaluation of research papers
conducted by Philip Goldberg,[17] six articles were attributed to male
authors for half of the subjects and to female authors for the other
half. The authorship of the articles was randomly assigned, and each
subject was asked to evaluate the scholarly merit of the article. Although the articles were identical except for the name of the author,
Goldberg found that those with male authorship were rated as better,
and a more significant contribution to knowledge, than those bearing
the name of a female. If we can assume that Goldberg's research is
applicable to many fields, male candidates may often have an advantage, even though the review committee has made a diligent effort to
review the work of all candidates.

One way of mitigating the possible effects of bias in evaluating
written work would be to institute a system of "blind" reviews: articles and (preferably) unpublished work could be circulated to members
of the review committee without the name of the candidate. When such
blind reviews are impractical, as they often are with senior appointments or in fields where authorship can easily be determined by subject matter, departments might request opinions from outside consultants. Alternatively, articles accepted by scholarly journals that have
a blind review process might be given more weight, as an indication
of the opinion of the professional community.

Judgments about women's intellectual competence also may be affected by unconscious stereotypes about the subject areas that attract
women. For example, in my own field of sociology it is often assumed
that women cannot (or will not) write "grand theory," and that women
gravitate toward "soft areas" of sociology—those involving personal
interaction and qualitative research—and shy away from large-scale
quantitative research.

Another widely held assumption in the field (which obviously con-
tradicts the previous one) is that women deal only with areas in which
they can manipulate finite data (quantitative research), such as
demography.[18] Whatever the parallel assumptions in other disciplines,
it is clear that these notions of women's specialties affect departmental
recruitment patterns and may work to eliminate serious consideration
of women candidates—when a department is looking for someone in a
theoretical specialty, it may exclude women candidates because of a
priori assumptions about women's aversion to theoretical work.

Finally, unconscious bias in selection standards involves assumptions about a woman's lack of commitment to her professional career, presumably because of family considerations. Often women professors are excluded from offers because it is assumed that they would not be "able" to move because of their husbands and/or children. In other cases, departments worry that a female professor with a family may not be as "available" to students, or may not spend as much time on departmental work. Commitment to one's family, interest in relocation, and availability to students vary greatly among academics—both men and women; it is both inaccurate and unfair to stereotype women in these ways. A priori assumptions about women's commitment can have a devastating effect on their careers, for they result in the exclusion of women from the normal opportunities for professional advancement. Furthermore, OFCC regulations specifically state that family status—both marriage and parenthood—is forbidden as a criterion of employment.

Overcoming established institutional patterns is as difficult as overcoming unconscious bias. Those committed to affirmative action changes often have felt that they were fighting the entire weight of the institutional structure in order to institute affirmative action goals. Cries of "academic freedom" and a backlash to affirmative action may be expected from those who have a vested interest in the status quo. Sheila Tobias, associate provost of Wesleyan University, analyzed the roots of this backlash and institutional resistance:

> During the sixties many universities previously independent of government support entered into contractual relations with federal agencies to do research. Since the bulk of the new money went for pure and applied scientific research, certain of the departments within the university were from the beginning indifferent or even hostile to the new sources of support. It is, in my view, no coincidence that the "backlash" to affirmative action, nation-wide, has come disproportionately from those departments which were in any case benefiting little from outside funding during the boom period and more importantly were losing power and prestige internally as a result. Thus, there is a mix of motives among those who find the university "vulgarized" by the hiring of women and minority members; they already regretted the federal support and the shift in power from old studies to new ones.
>
> Moreover there are three issues imbedded in the university hiring system that affirmative action has exposed:

1. The absence (or very low proportion, or unfair marginal hiring) of women and minority members from the faculty and therefore their absence from the hiring and promotion and tenure committees.
2. A system of hiring which was never open to scrutiny by many within the university and by no one without it. Promises of jobs were made often before jobs were officially announced. Senior professors could and did guarantee their colleagues jobs for the latter's best graduate protegees. Often no one supervised the recruitment process, the interviewing schedule, the selection decisions. University surveillance over promotion and tenure varied from department to department depending on the power relations enjoyed by the department chairman within the university. The kind of monitoring—not control, but monitoring—of the recruitment, interviewing and selection process, that came to be envisioned for a workable affirmative action plan, challenged some of these very old and cherished habits.
3. Reluctance to admit that "excellence" might be perceived narrowly. Even after a qualified candidate is brought to the campus, it is possible that sincere and honest members of a department will not recognize ability because it is wearing a skirt, or comes equipped with a high-pitched voice, or carries a "southern" accent; or because it is engaged in research that is not valued traditionally.

Each of these factors compounds the other, for until there is a sufficient number of women and non-whites on the faculty, there will be no discussion of the modes of perceiving excellence, nor any internal pressure to expand the recruiting network to include black universities and women's caucuses. By the same token, the successful recruitment of a critical mass of women and minority members in most departments will certainly generate such discussion and change. Affirmative action is, in the end, nothing more or less than a way of breaking into the vicious circle that causes the system to educate and to reward with jobs people just like those who are already there.[19]

Although we have argued that hiring on the basis of merit should enhance rather than impede academic freedom, those who have benefited from the old system may be expected to raise false issues to

forestall change. Because institutions are oriented toward stability
rather than change, and because it is always easier to do things the
"old way," the struggle to institute affirmative-action reforms will
continue to be a difficult one. It is clear that changes in basic institutional structures will be resisted and will require persistence, commitment, and endurance. However, two strategies may help: a
strong organization among those working for change, and a keen analysis of the institutional structure so that pressure is placed at the
right points. It is to these strategies that we now turn.

ACTION STRATEGIES FOR ACADEMIC WOMEN

In March 1972, I requested copies of affirmative action plans
from over 100 educational institutions, in preparation for a paper on
the effectiveness of current programs.[20] The list included all schools
that had submitted plans to HEW, and was supplemented by a national
list of educational institutions in order to review the full range of
programs at schools of differing sizes, regions, urbanity, sex ratio,
and prestige. I found that the effectiveness of the affirmative action
program was significantly related to two factors: the presence of a
women's group on campus and the experience of an HEW contract
compliance review. In brief, the schools with strong affirmative action programs had either an active women's group on campus or had
been visited by an HEW compliance team; schools with superior affirmative action programs had both. Of the schools with the lowest
ratings and, therefore, the least effective programs, only one had a
women's group and none had been investigated by HEW. While the
data obviously are incomplete, and the causal nature of the relationship cannot be proved, it does suggest the potential effectiveness of
strategic action by women. In all but two of the cases we studied,
the HEW compliance review was a result of a complaint by the women's
group or an individual woman.
    The first step in creating an active women's organization is get-
ting campus women together and developing awareness of common
problems. Some of the most successful groups originally were
formed as study groups to compile information on the status of women
at their university. Confronting the statistics is a powerful consciousness-raising device and provides hard data with which to confront
skeptics.
    One good example comes from my own experience. As part of
the American Sociological Association's Committee on the Status of
Women, I participated in a campus visit during which the committee
met informally with the entire department faculty. After a long discussion about the situation of women graduate students, the chairman

was asked the percentage who held research assistantships; he estimated that women held about half of both positions. When asked for
precise data, the chairman admitted he had never collected any. He
went down the list of courses, named each teaching assistant, and
then divided the total by sex: only 2 of the 20 were women. Both the
department chairman and the other faculty in the room were startled;
they had honestly not realized that the percentage was so low. They
were equally surprised and embarrassed when the data on research
positions were tabulated and showed an equally low figure. This experience of confronting the data was enough to convince most members
of the department of the need for more systematic attention to the experience of their female graduate students.

In organizing a group to compile data on the representation of
women faculty in various departments, it is important to include minority and staff women who can examine their respective situations.
Although female undergraduates, graduate students, staff, faculty,
and professionals may carry out separate research under the auspices
of numerous campus organizations, it is useful to have some campus-
wide coordination. At institutions where the level of consciousness
is very low, one organization may have to do the whole job.

Once the statistics have been compiled, it may be appropriate
to call a meeting of all university women to discuss the data and to
decide on a course of action. This action may take a number of forms.
First, a press conference should be called, the data reported, and a
suggestion of discrimination offered. If only a few women have worked
on compiling the data, a press conference may be held first and the
publicity used to call a meeting of all women to discuss the situation.
Another good publicity-getting device is filing a complaint with HEW
or EEOC.* (A press conference is useful here also.) In order to file
a complaint with HEW, it is not necessary to prepare formal charges
or to have a wealth of statistics—a letter to the Secretary of Labor
alleging unfair treatment of women constitutes a formal complaint.
However, it often is useful to have data documenting women's exclusion to convince both the university administration and skeptics of
the legitimacy of the women's case. The next or concurrent step is,
of course, to form action groups and to recommend concrete proposals
for change. It may be helpful for university women to draw up their
own affirmative action plan; it can then serve as a basis for negotiation with administrators and forces recognition of key problem areas.
Once action proposals are agreed upon, representatives of women's
groups should meet with university officials and ask them to initiate
the action requested.

---

*The Equal Employment Opportunities Commission gained juris-
diction over academic employees in March 1972.

In dealing with a university administration, women's groups must protect their members from reprisals. There have been numerous complaints from university women across the country who feel that their contracts have been terminated because of political activity in women's groups. For example, the women at the University of Pittsburgh are seeking court action against the university for firing the leaders of the women's caucus.

Women's groups can protect their members in several ways. No individual should be designated as "the" spokeswoman for a group; chairpersons and representatives who meet with administrators should be rotated. In dealing with the press, a group identification is essential—many names should be listed and individuals referred to only as "spokeswomen" for the group. All signed documents should have as many names as possible. It also is important to ensure that university officials and administrators are never visited by single individuals; they should always be seen by a group. This practice has three advantages: first, the presence of a sufficient number of witnesses precludes the possibility of a misstatement by the administrator concerning what was said; second, it precludes the possibility of a single individual's being labeled a neurotic or a troublemaker or being personally threatened; third, it has psychological power—many men are afraid of confronting a room full of women. In short, a group shows that many women share these concerns, and that they cannot be dismissed as the complaint of a single "troublemaker."

Finally, in writing letters, meeting with administrators, and holding press conferences, the assistance of senior women faculty can be especially helpful. A woman with tenure is much less vulnerable to administrative reprisals, and can add legitimacy and authority to women's actions. Even if these women are too busy to participate fully, they may be willing to give permission to use their names in letters and press releases.

It is especially important for women's groups to understand the real power structure of their universities, as a keen analysis of the institutional structure is essential to effective pressure for change. In some schools the president makes decisions, while in others it may be a provost or dean who can institute crucial affirmative action programs.

It also is important that women's groups be organized on various levels. In some departments a women's caucus may be necessary to bring female candidates to the attention of the recruitment committee, or to ensure equal distribution of research funds. In others, women graduate students may have to protest fellowship awards to change department policies. However, faculty women should not define their concerns too narrowly; they may be of crucial assistance in providing equal treatment for graduate student women. Similarly, it often may be easier for graduate student women to argue for improvements in the situation of women faculty. Black and Chicano women may want to organize separately to deal with their unique concerns, but mutual support and assistance should bind all women's groups together.

A careful study of university regulations also may prove helpful. If existing regulations prohibiting discriminatory practices are not being enforced, they can be called to the attention of the person responsible. For example, placement offices often ignore their own guidelines that they should not accept discriminatory job listings. If a change in practice does not result from a direct informative request, women may effect very rapid change by publicizing the violation of current regulations.

Although it is important to try to work within the university, and to negotiate directly with the university administration, many women's groups have found that they are being ignored by those with power to effect change. Therefore, it is essential that women marshal external resources to put pressure on the university administration. Even when there are some conciliatory efforts by the administration, external pressure can greatly affect both the degree and speed of its response to the women's proposals. The five most significant outside resources available to university women are the press, alumnae, political pressure, HEW, and the courts.

The press can provide women with a very powerful weapon against a recalcitrant university administration. A report in the local newspaper of charges of sex discrimination, the filing of a complaint with HEW, or the refusal of a university president to meet with a women's group or to take specific action (such as establishing a day care center or correcting salary inequities) clearly is feared by most university administrators. Because educational institutions are sensitive to such adverse publicity, they may become more responsive and receptive to the suggestions of women's groups. Another way to get press coverage is to have a national feminist speaker discuss local issues after a campus lecture. For example, when Gloria Steinem came to Yale, she spoke to the press (at the request of local women) about Mory's, the exclusive eating club that still discriminated against women at the time.

Appeals to alumnae provide another source of external pressure. Women's groups might consider a mailing to all university alumnae requesting that they withhold their contributions until sex discrimination is eliminated; in some cases, just the threat of this action is effective. Distributing leaflets to visiting alumnae groups to explain grievances against the administration, and letters to the Board of Trustees or to active alumnae groups, are other potential sources of support.

Writing to and visiting state and local legislators, or the governor (if the school is a state-supported institution), also may prove ef-

fective. Further, state Congressmen and Senators can be of great
assistance in putting pressure on federally funded institutions and in
speeding up compliance reviews.

The threat of an HEW compliance review is a very strong source
of support in bargaining with a university administration. If a review
is scheduled, women should try to make sure that it receives a maxi-
mum amount of publicity, that rallies and public meetings are held
during the course of the review, and that there is some provision for
women to meet privately with HEW investigators (preferably off the
university campus).

It should be noted, however, that women's groups that have hoped
for strong enforcement pressures from HEW often have been disap-
pointed. HEW seems to have neither the inclination nor the resources
to effectively and consistently enforce affirmative action regulations.
Some compliance reviews have been glaringly inadequate; and no university contract has been terminated by HEW, nor have any termination hearings been held. HEW has suffered from an inadequate compliance staff and the difficulties of extracting personnel information
from recalcitrant universities. Some universities have been almost
unbelievably uncooperative. HEW officials have then argued that they
cannot proceed to cancel contracts or hold up new ones without clear
mathematical proof that discrimination exists. Nonetheless, it would
seem that failure to provide required personnel data would constitute
a rather serious failure to comply. Apparently HEW is simply afraid
or not committed enough to use the sanctions at its disposal.

The universities and HEW also have been accused of subverting
affirmative action in other ways. For example, rumors have persis-
ted that at the University of Michigan some new contracts were signed,
and some new projects expected in the form of contracts were processed
as grants, during the period from October through December 1970,
when HEW had placed a hold on the signing of new contracts. In regard to such maneuvers, a regional civil rights staff member has
noted that contract officers both in the university and in government
are adept at dodging holds. Typically, contracts are simply kept on
desks until holds are lifted. By not submitting documents for signing,
the issue of discrimination and noncompliance can be avoided, at least
temporarily.

It also is clear that political pressure has affected HEW's Office
for Civil Rights in various ways. For example, compliance reviews
at both Harvard and Yale have been inexplicably interrupted and de-
layed. It also is difficult to understand why a large portion of the
academically oriented and experienced New England compliance staff
was suddenly required to conduct compliance reviews of construction
firms. In addition, the sex-discrimination guidelines for universities
were held up for over two years, undergoing constant reformulation,
before they were issued.

Finally, the contracting officers in federal agencies vary in their commitment. Some bring pressure to bear on university officials to comply with HEW, but others are simply interested in business as usual. It is clear that if affirmative action is to become a reality, academic women will have to continue their relentless efforts to force the universities and HEW into upholding and enforcing federal law.

The ultimate resource available to university women is now the courts. Following the educational amendments of 1972, academic women are covered by Title VII of the Civil Rights Act (administered by the Equal Employment Opportunities Commission) and by the Equal Pay Act of 1963 (administered by the Wage and Hours Division of the Department of Labor). Both of these acts have much stronger enforcement mechanisms than the executive order, both agencies are better staffed and more vigorous in enforcing compliance than HEW has been, and both allow for individual remedies (such as reinstatement and back pay) instead of the more remote sanctions of withholding contracts. Individual grievances probably will receive a speedier and more effective hearing through EEOC or the Wage and Hours Division than if they await an HEW compliance review. If the case goes to court, the plaintiffs will have the strong legal force of a court order for reinstatement, salary increase, or back pay. When an individual does use EEOC or Wage and Hours, local women can benefit from the case by insisting that the decision be well publicized and that similar inequities be corrected immediately.

Although the most effective strategy for each university will depend on situational factors, in general we can conclude that continuous internal and external pressure by women's groups will result in a more rigorous affirmative action program. Without such pressure there is little indication of anything but stagnation and regression, but with it there is hope for the future.

NOTES

1. Office of Civil Rights, U.S. Department of Health, Education and Welfare, "Higher Education Guidelines for Executive Order 11246," October 1, 1972, p. 3. Hereafter cited as HEW Guidelines.

2. Office of Federal Contract Compliance, U.S. Department of Labor, "Affirmative Action Programs" (commonly referred to as order no. 4), Federal Register 36 #(234), p. 23152 (1971); Title 4 Code of Federal Regulations, Chapter 60, Sections 1 and 2.

3. HEW Guidelines, pp. 16-17.

4. OFCC Regulations, §60-2.24 F5.

5. HEW Guidelines, p. 9.

6. OFCC Regulations, §60-2.24b.

7. HEW Guidelines, p. 4.

8. OFCC Regulations, $60-2.24F5.

9. HEW Guidelines, p. 7.

10. Ibid.

11. Ibid., p. 8.

12. Ibid., p. 9.

13. Ibid.

14. Ibid., p. 11.

15. Helen S. Astin and Alan E. Bayer, "Sex Discrimination in Academe," in Alice S. Rossi and Ann Calderwood, eds., Academic Women on the Move (New York: Russell Sage Foundation, 1973), pp. 333-56. Astin and Bayer provide an excellent review of the data on sex differentials in rank, salary, and academic tenure.

16. OFCC Regulations, $60-2.24; HEW Guidelines, p. 14.

17. Philip Goldberg, "Are Women Prejudiced Against Women?" Transaction 5 (April 1968): 28-30.

18. Alice S. Rossi, "Status of Women in Graduate Departments of Sociology," The American Sociologist 5, no. 1 (February 1970).

19. Sheila Tobias, "Affirmative Action for Women in the Universities, Why All the Fuss?" Radcliffe Quarterly, December 1974, pp. 14-16.

20. For a discussion of the results, see Lenore J. Weitzman, "Affirmative Action Plans for Eliminating Sex Discrimination in Academe," in Academic Women on the Move, p. 463.

6

DEVELOPING CRITERIA
AND MEASURES OF
EQUAL OPPORTUNITIES
FOR WOMEN
Elizabeth L. Scott

The criteria and measures needed to determine whether women have equal opportunities, and the goals and programs set up to provide equal opportunities, are necessarily largely statistical. Fear of recrimination and doubts about the relative importance of lack of ability and discrimination rule out the alternative possibility of using personal histories.

The affirmative action programs arising as a result of HEW regulations impose statistical criteria. The federal orders mandate the development of goals and timetables to remedy the underutilization of women, where underutilization is defined as having fewer women in a particular job or pay category than would reasonably be expected by their availability in the work force. We shall discuss briefly the difficulties in obtaining the data needed to construct appropriate goals, and then provide suggestions for improving the data needed for long-range goals.

Short-range goals and timetables are more difficult to set up because there is the additional requirement that they be attainable in the time prescribed. Nevertheless, they are required and may be useful. We shall provide several tentative proposals for the construction and surveillance of short-range timetables for women in academia, both for appointments and for salaries.

Next we shall consider another phenomenon. Certain employers tend to discount the possibility of appointing or promoting women rather than men, even when there are moral and legal pressures to

---

This chapter was prepared with the partial support of the National Institute of Health and the Carnegie Commission on Higher Education.

appoint women and even though a "data bank" of biobibliographies of trained women has been established. The claim may be that women suffer when compared with men on the basis of such criteria as aptitude, creativity in science, attrition, or general intelligence. We shall point to several studies indicating that academic women compare equally well, or better than, academic men in these attributes—contrary to popular belief. These studies are not conclusive, but they may help to build a buffer against old beliefs and to aid in changing attitudes.

Lastly, realizing that long-range goals and a change of attitudes will be difficult to achieve and slow at best, we shall suggest several programs that can be instituted immediately. Each of these programs will ease the progress toward equal opportunities for women in academia. Indeed, initiating them might be considered one of the first criteria to be met in achieving this goal.

LONG-RANGE GOALS

The development of goals and timetables to remedy the underutilization of women first requires a knowledge of the number of men and the number of women now employed in each job category, together with information on their salaries, responsibilities, training, and experience. Also required is a knowledge of the corresponding figures for men and women available in the work force, employed or not. These data should be further subdivided by race.

Unfortunately, the data to be used are, for the most part, poor. Often they are entirely missing or are not available because they are classified as confidential. These problems are particularly severe in academe; at best the statistics are incomplete. What can be done? The answer seems to be either to estimate the statistics needed, or to state that no suitable women are available. Since we know of no category in which the second answer is strictly true, let us look at the first.*

The statistics provided by the Bureau of the Census for the Standard Metropolitan Statistical Area (SMSA) provide a breakdown of the overall working population in the area by sex and by racial/ethnic group. As an example, suppose the SMSA is

*I am indebted to Madeline Mixer, head of the Women's Bureau, Western Region, Department of Labor; to James Meto, regional manpower consultant, HRD; to several experts within the University of California; and to the authors of several affirmative action programs for discussions of the details of what actually is being done to obtain the estimates needed.

73 percent white, of whom 38 percent are women and
   62 percent are men
18 percent black, of whom 53 percent are women and
   47 percent are men
 2 percent Oriental, of whom 51 percent are women and
   49 percent are men
 7 percent Spanish surname, of whom 37 percent are women and
   63 percent are men.

These racial/ethnic percentages are superimposed over the entire job categories grid. Thus, the long-range goal for every employer is that eventually about 73 percent of the officials and managers shall be white, 18 percent black, 2 percent Oriental, and 7 percent Spanish surname. This same pattern is set as a goal for the professional staff, technicians, clerical workers, craftsmen, laborers, and service workers. In academe there usually are further subdivisions in the same pattern.

The goals for equal employment opportunities for women are then computed within each racial group. That is, we have supposed that 38 percent of the white workers are women. Then 38 percent of the white officials and managers shall be women and 62 percent men, 38 percent of the white professionals shall eventually be women, and so on. Since we supposed that among black workers 53 percent are women, among Orientals 51 percent, and among Spanish-surnamed 37 percent, this information is also applied to the job category grid to obtain long-range goals: 73 x .38 = 28 percent of employees in each job category shall eventually be white women, 18 x .53 = 10 percent shall be black women, 2 x .51 = 1 percent Oriental women, and 7 x .37 = 3 percent Spanish-surnamed women.

The employment patterns of women are changing rather rapidly. This means that the SMSA is no longer applicable even when the 1970 census details become available. As the decade goes on, the SMSA is less reliable. It is now well established that the census data appreciably underestimate the numbers of minorities and of women in the work force, but the exact amount of error is not known.

Clearly, even for long-range goals more precise data are needed. The federal agencies are aware of this need, but there are no immediate plans to obtain the data. For example, in a recent employer survey made by HRD, the schedules in the field showed neither race nor sex, only jobs by classification. The purpose of the survey was to project total occupational needs for vocational training, not to provide data for goals in employment. Nevertheless, the Manpower Development Training Program has 60 percent "disadvantaged," a term indicating minority race and women as well as low educational level.

Employers will say that the long-range goals computed above, even with precise figures, are not realistic for now—women must be found, recruited, and trained for the job categories in which women are underutilized. The federal orders mandate recruitment and training programs, but they can be expected to proceed slowly. However, they will provide another source of statistics on the availability of women for specified job categories.

Women also will say that the long-range goals computed above are not realistic. As shown in Figure 6.1, percentages of women in the labor force increase markedly with educational level: a mere 24 percent of women who have less than eight years' education are in the labor force and only 31 percent of those with eight years schooling. The percentage in the labor force jumps to 40 percent of those with one-three years of high school and to 48 percent of those with four years of high school; with higher education the percentages start at 45 percent of those with one-three years of college and climb to 54 percent with four years, to 71 percent with five or more years, and to 91 percent of those receiving the Ph.D. in 1958-63. On the other hand, the percentages for men in the labor force are high at every educational level. For women, it is not correct to apply an overall figure for the proportion of women in the labor force; the better-educated the woman, the more likely she is to be in the labor force and available for those job categories requiring more education. But the proportion of women obtaining higher degrees decreases rapidly with the level of the degree, especially in some fields, so the situation today is complex. For the long-range goal, women will have to be recruited and encouraged to undertake advanced education and training.

It is clear that data need to be collected to allow the establishment of realistic goals for minorities and for women. These can indeed start with the details available in the 1970 census but ordinarily not published. But, even so, the census will not provide such detailed information as is needed to establish and to correct discrimination at each level in academia. The universities have to provide this information themselves. Many have started to do so; help and encouragement—perhaps even compulsion—are needed to complete the studies. Moreover, these studies can be used first to establish short-range goals.

SHORT-RANGE GOALS

It is important that short-range goals be attainable. The data for them should be derived from the actual recruiting area for the category. In some categories in academia this appears to be possible. Let us consider the University of California at Berkeley. We suggest

FIGURE 6.1

Labor Force Participation Rates of Women, by Educational Level, March 1968
(age 18 and over)

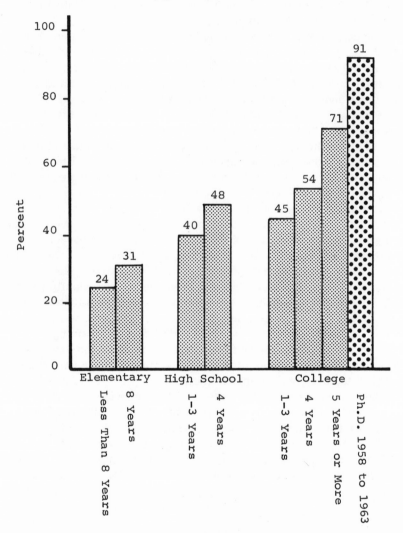

Sources: Rita J. Simon et al., "Women Ph.D.: A Recent Pro-file," in Social Problems 15 (1967): 221-36; "Trends in Educational Attainment of Women," U.S. Department of Labor, Wage and Labor Standards Administration, October 1969, p. 9.

TABLE 6.1

Number of Doctorates Given in 1964-65, 1965-66, and 1967-68, by Field and Sex in
the First Five and the First Ten Distinguished Departments for That Field, Rated by
Quality of Graduate Faculty, in Comparison with Berkeley

Field	"First Five" Number Men	Women	Per-cent Women	"First Ten" Number Men	Women	Per-cent Women	Berkeley Ph.D's Percent Women Same 3 Yrs.	5 Yrs. 1962-67	Berkeley Faculty, Percent Women
Anthropology	100	26	20.6	155	40	20.5	27.0	17.4	13.2
Astronomy	57	8	12.3	85	11	11.5	7.7	4.0	0.0
Biochemistry	108	20	15.6	158	34	17.7	14.7	13.3	0.0
Chemistry	362	27	6.9	814	73	8.2	8.1	4.8	0.0
Economics	291	23	7.3	477	35	6.8	11.7	5.6	0.0
Engineering	1,118	2	0.2	1,738	4	0.2	0.0	0.0	0.0
English	368	99	21.2	591	176	22.9	25.5	22.5	4.3
French	58	37	38.8	93	50	58.9	19.2	16.1	1.9
German	36	13	25.6	70	21	23.1	0.0	7.0	23.3
History	408	54	11.7	564	91	13.0	6.2	10.8	0.0
Mathematics	288	15	5.0	501	31	5.8	5.1	3.4	0.0
Philosophy	105	8	7.1	191	16	7.7	7.1	4.8	5.6
Physics	422	11	2.5	819	22	2.6	2.4	1.4	0.0
Physiology-Anatomy	30	9	23.1	82	24	22.9	22.2	9.1	13.3
Political Science	247	34	12.1	356	47	11.7	8.3	4.2	0.9
Psychology	256	81	24.0	443	130	22.7	34.1	27.7	0.0
Sociology	116	37	24.2	199	51	20.4	29.2	23.5	0.0
Spanish, Portuguese	44	16	26.5	66	34	33.9	19.2	16.1	7.3
Zoology	96	40	29.4	229	70	23.4	21.6	15.2	0.0

Source: E. Colson, E. I. Scott, H. Blumer, S. Ervin-Tripp, and F. Newman,
"Report of the Subcommittee on the Status of Academic Women on the Berkeley Campus" (Berkeley: Academic Senate, University of California, 1970), pp. 1-78.

FIGURE 6.2

Percentage of Women Among Undergraduate Majors, Graduate Majors, Doctoral Degrees, and Faculty, University of California, 1966–69

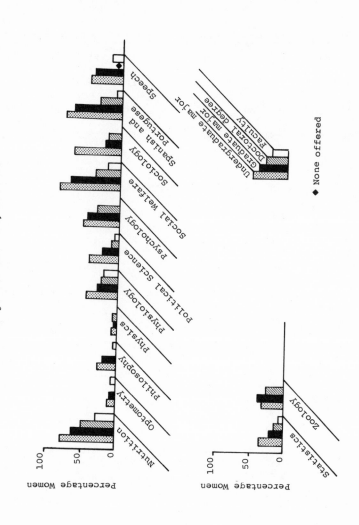

Note: These are ladder positions, excluding nonteaching emeriti, for selected departments.

Source: E. Colson, E. L. Scott, H. Blumer, S. Ervin-Tripp, and F. Newman, "Report of the Subcommittee on the Status of Academic Women on the Berkeley Campus," The Academic Senate, University of California, 1970, p. 18.

FIGURE 6.3

Percentage of Women Among Undergraduates, Graduates, Ladder Faculty, and Professors in Various Fields

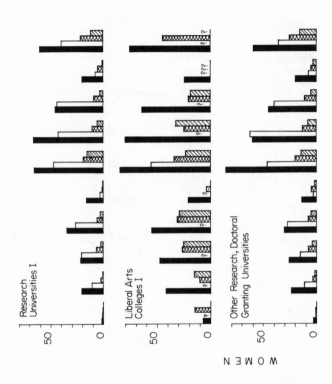

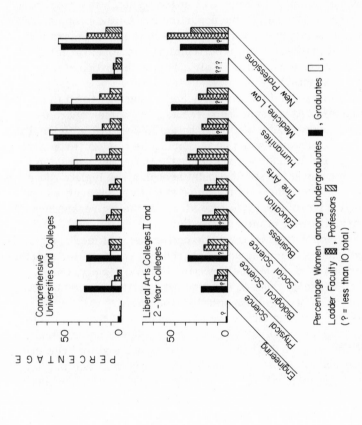

Note: ? = less than 10 total.

Source: Martin A. Trow, "Appendix—Carnegie Commission on Higher Education National Survey of Faculty and Student Opinion," in Martin A. Trow, ed., Teachers and Students (New York: McGraw-Hill, 1975).

that the proportion of women among assistant professors in a specified field should at least be as great as the proportion of women among
Ph.D.'s in the five (or ten) most prestigious departments in that field
over the last three years. It is from this crop of Ph.D.'s that almost
all appointments at Berkeley are made. There are many women available in almost every field, as Table 6.1 shows. Clearly, to bring
the ratio of women assistant professors at Berkeley to the level of the
ratio of women Ph.D.'s would require that quite a number of women
be appointed. We suggest that this policy be continued until the proportion of women assistant professors at least equals the proportion
of women graduate students in the department. As the proportion of
women graduate students grows, so will the expected proportion of
women assistant professors. (In our opinion, the appearance of women assistant professors will in itself increase the proportion of women graduate students.)

As Figure 6.2 indicates, Berkeley has a long way to go to achieve
equal proportions. At present the percentage of women decreases
strikingly from undergraduates to graduates to doctorates to faculty,
so that the percentage of women on the faculty is tiny, or even zero,
in almost every field. This strong decrease in the percentage of
women at each successive step extends through all of higher education
and is especially pronounced in the more selective universities and
colleges. (See Figure 6.3.) We note also that the representation of
women is very different in the various fields.

University appointments are made on the basis of merit; expectations of excellence in teaching and research are required for appointment, and evidence of such excellence is required for promotion.
For example, Berkeley tries to get the best. Will Berkeley be lowering its standards of quality by appointing women? Or can Berkeley
raise its quality by taking advantage of a larger pool from which to
select students and a much larger pool from which to select faculty?
This is a touchy subject that requires more study, and we urge that
the studies be made. Still, we show below strong evidence that the inclusion of more women will tend to increase quality in higher education.

ATTAINING EQUAL SALARY OPPORTUNITIES
FOR WOMEN

Not only are women underrepresented on university and college
faculties, but those women who are employed receive lower salaries,
on the average, than men. However, a smaller percentage of faculty
women than men have a doctorate, and their age distributions are different. To what extent are the differences in salary due to differen-

ces in ability and in performance, and to what extent are they the result of discrimination? If men and women of the same ability and performance receive different salaries, this should be corrected immediately.

We studied this question, using the large-scale national survey made by the Carnegie Commission on Higher Education in the spring of 1969 in cooperation with the Office of Research of the American Council on Education. A comprehensive questionnaire was returned by 60,028 faculty members spread among 78 universities, 168 four-year colleges, and 57 two-year colleges. H. S. Astin and A. E. Bayer used a linear regression equation with 32 predictor variables to compare the salary a woman would receive with that of a man having the same rank, background, and achievements.[1] They concluded that the actual amount of discrimination exceeds $1,040 in annual salary and one-fifth step in rank. We decided to extend the study by Astin and Bayer to investigate the salary differences between men and women for different types of institution and different fields separately, since we suspected that the salary differences would be larger in some types of institution and field than in others. We also hoped thereby to get better estimates. In addition, we included higher-order interaction terms in the salary predictors and, we believe, did a better job handling part-time faculty. (The survey neglected to ask whether employment is full-time; Astin and Bayer eliminated all persons teaching less than nine hours per week, but that cut out most of the faculty in the selective institutions and, overall, eliminated 51 percent of the men and 35 percent of the women sampled.)

Our analyses were based on the replies of all women sampled and a 25 percent random sample of the men. The studies were done separately by type of institution, field, and sex. We estimated whether a faculty member held a part-time appointment from his answers to a battery of questions. Both full-time and part-time employees were included in the analyses, and the reduction in salary due to part-time employment was estimated. Table 6.2 summarizes the results for the combined fields of biological and physical sciences in the category Research Universities I. The predictor variables, such as sex, date of birth, and number of books, are listed briefly. The same predictor variables are used for each type-field classification but their importance varies, as is indicated by the changes in the values of the corresponding coefficients and their significance levels. The complete set of coefficients is given in Table 6.3. These tables allow us to estimate, by a simple additive equation using 26 predictor variables, including 3 interaction terms, the salary that a man would receive and the salary that a woman would receive for each type of institution and each field. These estimated salaries

TABLE 6.2

Coefficients of the Multilinear Regression Equation for Predicting Faculty Salaries, Research Universities I, Biological and Physical Sciences

	Men and Women	Men	Women	Variable
Constant	2.62	2.21	-.06	
1	-.60[c]	—	—	Sex: 1 = male, 2 = female
2	.11[a]	.12	.15[a]	Date of birth: 1 = 1908 or before, to 9 = 1944 or later
3	.23	.13	-.24	Marital status: 1 = never married, 2 = married or formerly married
4	.40[c]	.21[b]	.46[a]	Number of children: 1 = none, to 4 = three or more
5	.73[c]	.80[c]	.73[c]	Highest degree: 0 = B.A. or less, 1 = M.A., 2 = doctorate
6	-.15[c]	-.16[c]	-.10[a]	Year of highest degree: 11 = 1928 or before, to 21 = 1967 or later
7	.12	.11	.07	B.A. from a prestigious school: 0 = no, 1 = yes
8	-.12	-.08	-.32[b]	Graduate degree from a prestigious school: 0 = no, 1 = yes
9	.07	.08	.00	Support toward highest degree: 0 = none, to 2 = teaching/research assistantship plus fellowship
10	—	—	—	Rank (variable omitted)
11	.23[c]	.26[c]	.15[a]	Years employed in academe: 1 = one or less, to 8 = 30 or more
12	-.13[c]	-.15[c]	-.09	Years employed in present institution: 1 = one or less, to 8 = 30 or more
13	-.07	-.09[a]	.04	Quality of present institution: 1 = high, to 7 = low
14	.40[c]	.37[c]	.44[c]	Number of articles: 1 = none, to 6 = more than 20
15	.13[b]	.10[a]	.19	Number of books: 1 = none, to 4 = five or more
16	.06	.08	.00	Association with a research institute: 1 = yes, 2 = no
17	.03	.01	.20[a]	Number of sources of research support: 0 to 6

#				Variable
18	.25[c]	.23[c]	.36[a]	Number of sources of paid consulting: 0 to 6
19	−.08[a]	−.12[a]	.02	Research/teaching inclination: 1 = heavily research, to 4 = heavily teaching
20	.19[c]	.20[c]	.12[a]	Administrative activity: 1 = none, to 7 = 81 to 100 percent time
21	.01	.02	−.03	Consulting: 1 = none, to 7 = 81 to 100 percent time
22	−.10[a]	−.10[a]	−.16	Outside professional practice: 1 = none, to 7 = 81 to 100 percent time
23	−.13[c]	−.15[c]	−.01	Hours taught per week, 1 = none, to 9 = 21 or more
24	.78[c]	.78[c]	.84[c]	Salary base: 1 = 9/10 months, 2 = 11/12 months
27	.04[c]	.03[b]	−.06[c]	Interaction: date of birth and number of articles
28	−.11	−.11	—	Interaction: sex and number of children
29	−.03[b]	−.03	−.08[a]	Interaction: date of birth and number of children
30	.03	.17[a]	.10	Interaction: sex, marital status, and age: 1 = male, never married, under 30, to 8 = female, married or formerly married, 30 years or older
31	−.69[c]	−.69[c]	−.42[b]	Part-time by Rule 5: 1 = full-time, 2 = part-time

Salary range: 1 = below $7,000, to 9 = $30,000 or more; one interval is $3,000 (or $2,000 or $5,000)

[a]Individual coefficient differs from zero at 0.05 significance level (two-sided).
[b]Differs at 0.01 level.
[c]Differs at 0.001 level.

Note: Study covered 1,183 men and 312 women.

Source: Martin A. Trow, "Appendix—Carnegie Commission on Higher Education National Survey of Faculty and Student Opinion," in Martin A. Trow, ed., Teachers and Students (New York: McGraw-Hill, 1975).

95

TABLE 6.3

Coefficients of the Multilinear Regression Equation for Predicting
Faculty Salaries in Research Universities I

Predictors	Field: Sex:	Biological/Phy- sical Science		Education	
		Men	Women	Men	Women
Constant		2.21	-.06	2.34	5.19
2 Date of birth		.12	.15[a]	-.02	-.05
3 Marital status		.13	-.24	.08	-.14
4 No. of child.		.21[b]	.46[a]	.18	.11
5 Highest degree		.80[c]	.73[c]	.86[c]	.76[c]
6 Year of degree		-.16[c]	-.10[a]	-.11[a]	-.14[c]
7 B.A. prestigious		.11	.07	-.04	-.09
8 Graduate prest.		-.08	-.32[b]	-.15	.12
9 Support		.08	.00	-.01	-.04
11 Years academe		.26[c]	.15[a]	.12	.11[a]
12 Years present		-.15[c]	-.09	-.06	-.07
13 Qual. present		-.09[a]	.04	.05	.08
14 No. articles		.37[c]	.44[c]	.19	.14[a]
15 No. books		.10[a]	.19	.10	-.02
16 Assoc. research		.08	-.00	-.18	-.04
17 No. research		.01	.20[a]	.17[a]	.13
18 No. consulting		.23[c]	.36[a]	.25[c]	.19[c]
19 Research/Teach.		-.12[a]	.02	-.01	-.08
20 Administrative		.20[c]	.12[a]	.09[a]	.13[c]
21 Consulting		.02	-.03	-.08	-.12[a]
22 Prof. practice		-.10[a]	-.16	.09	-.03
23 Hours taught		-.15[c]	-.01	-.15[c]	-.14[c]
24 Salary base		.78[c]	.84[c]	1.02[c]	.52[c]
27 Birth x no. art.		-.03[b]	-.06[c]	-.02	-.01
29 Birth x no. child.		-.03	-.08[a]	-.03	-.02
30 Sex x mar. x age		.17[a]	.10	.10	-.03
31 Part-time		-.69[c]	-.42[b]	-.34[a]	-.65[c]
No. observations		1,183	312	320	381
No. variables		26	26	26	26
Res'l. d.f.		1,156	285	293	354
Multiple R-squared		.71	.69	.69	.70
Res'l. mean square		1.16	.92	1.00	.63
Mean opp. sex res'l.		1.17	-1.04	.58	-.48
S.D. opp. sex res'l.		1.19	1.12	1.06	.94

	Fine Arts		Humanities		Social Science		New Professions	
	Men	Women	Men	Women	Men	Women	Men	Women
8.01	3.27	3.27	3.92	5.18	2.54	5.48	2.56	
-.02	-.05	.04	-.08[a]	-.01	-.07	-.04	-.04	
.23	.10	.02	-.08	.05	-.21	.16	-.16	
.27	-.20	.22[b]	-.29[a]	.33[b]	-.21	.16	-.12	
.51[c]	.68[c]	.45[c]	.33[c]	.52[c]	.49[b]	.48[c]	.68[c]	
-.25[c]	-.09[a]	-.15[c]	-.01	-.18[c]	-.07	-.18[c]	-.07[c]	
-.08	.05	.01	-.01	-.01	.02	.05	.17[a]	
.14	-.20	.23[b]	.08	-.11	.06	-.04	.00	
-.02	-.04	.10	.07	.02	-.04	.11	.03	
.09	.15	.29[c]	.13[c]	.24[c]	.27[b]	.01	.13[c]	
-.01	-.05	-.12[c]	-.03	-.13[c]	-.13	-.08	-.06[a]	
-.19	-.34[b]	.10	-.12[a]	.16[a]	.01	-.22[a]	-.08	
.03	.17	.27[c]	.18[b]	.31[c]	.10	.16[a]	.23[c]	
.08	.07	.34[c]	.26[c]	.04	.11	.21[c]	.05	
-.21	.10	-.07	-.17	-.09	-.08	-.14	-.03	
.05	.09	.02	.13	.00	.02	.03	.18[c]	
.27[b]	.08	.09	.18[b]	.15[c]	.07	.21[c]	.19[c]	
-.14	-.00	-.09	-.06	-.16[b]	.08	-.09	.03	
.16[b]	.13	.16[c]	.16[c]	.14[c]	.19[b]	.22[c]	.18[c]	
-.08	-.01	-.14[b]	-.02	.06	.07	-.13[b]	.01	
-.14[b]	-.01	-.13[a]	-.19[c]	-.21[c]	.01	-.31[c]	-.09[a]	
-.06	.02	-.12[c]	-.17[c]	-.18[c]	-.09	-.03	-.05[c]	
.34[a]	.26	.28[c]	-.01	.63[c]	.56[c]	.96[c]	.52[c]	
.01	-.03	-.02[a]	-.01	-.02	.02	-.00	-.02	
-.06[a]	.03	-.03	.04	-.04[a]	.03	-.02	.01	
.02	-.06	.06	-.01	-.00	.03	.08	.02	
-.89[c]	-.29	-.38[c]	-.72[c]	-.54[c]	-.23	-.60[c]	-.31[c]	
264	192	712	520	581	215	700	1,029	
26	26	26	26	26	26	26	26	
237	165	685	493	554	188	673	1,002	
.69	.60	.78	.70	.73	.56	.60	.63	
.99	.71	.84	.50	.94	1.11	1.39	.83	
.84	-.77	.72	-.58	.97	-.50	.79	-.69	
1.17	.99	1.11	.87	1.11	1.10	1.28	1.06	

(continued)

TABLE 6.3 (continued)

Coefficients of the Multilinear Regression Equation for Predicting
Faculty Salaries in Research Universities II and Doctoral Granting
Universities I and II

Predictors	Field: Sex:	Biological/Physical Science		Education	
		Men	Women	Men	Women
Constant		3.47	-.35	3.00	2.98
2 Date of birth		.02	.09	-.12	-.13^b
3 Marital status		-.23	-.19	-.02	-.03
4 No. of child.		.28^c	.57^b	.16	-.35
5 Highest degree		.77^c	.63^c	.54^c	.49^c
6 Year of degree		-.15^c	-.05	-.11^a	.03
7 B.A. prestigious		.12	.05	.19	.07
8 Graduate prest.		.12	.08	.09	.05
9 Support		.02	-.04	-.00	.10
11 Years academe		.23^c	.17^b	-.01	.08
12 Years present		-.16^c	-.09	-.04	-.03
13 Qual. present		.03	.03	.07	-.05
14 No. articles		.27^c	.41^c	.32^c	.21^b
15 No. books		.15^b	.31^a	.25^c	.04
16 Assoc. research		.03	.03	.04	-.20
17 No. research		.01	.04	-.03	.13
18 No. consulting		.17^c	.11	.14^b	.07
19 Research/Teach.		-.08	-.06	-.13	-.02
20 Administrative		.21^c	.21^c	.12^c	.06^a
21 Consulting		.09	.05	-.07	-.05
22 Prof. practice		-.21^c	-.08	-.19^b	-.13^b
23 Hours taught		-.12^c	-.05	-.05	-.09^c
24 Salary base		.69^c	.72^c	1.10^c	.43^c
27 Birth x no. art.		-.02^a	-.03	-.03	-.01
29 Birth x no. child.		-.03^c	-.10^b	-.01	.04
30 Sex x mar. x age		-.03	.04	.05	.01
31 Part-time		-.46^c	-.37	-.09	-.48^b
No. observations		941	254	368	468
No. variables		26	26	26	26
Res'l. d.f.		914	227	341	441
Multiple R-squared		.69	.64	.67	.55
Res'l. mean square		.87	.84	.83	.79
Mean Opp. sex res'l.		.60	-.34	.84	-.50
S.D. opp. sex res'l.		.98	.93	1.07	1.04

	Fine Arts		Humanities		Social Science		New Professions	
	Men	Women	Men	Women	Men	Women	Men	Women
1.28	2.84	2.07	1.31	5.17	.80	2.48	1.21
-.09	-.17^b	-.05	.00	-.03	.05	-.08	-.04
-.12	.08	.41^b	-.22^a	-.13	-.58	.80^b	-.31^a
.27	-.15	.18^a	-.11	.17	-.47^a	.18	-.08
-.01	.57^c	.34^c	.34^c	.79^c	.46^b	.77^c	.78^c
.06	-.02	-.03	.00	-.19^c	.07	-.13^c	-.02
.16	.36	.07	.09	-.23^a	.09	-.18	.08
.18	-.21	.24^b	.10	.11	.14	.28^a	-.03
-.01	.09	-.00	.03	.15	-.13	.03	.01
.24^c	.12	.36^c	.10^b	.18^c	.33^c	.06	.12^c
-.03	-.03	-.11^c	.05	-.20^c	-.29^c	-.03	-.01
-.01	-.24	-.01	.02	.01	-.07	-.16	.02
.06	.10	.15^b	.56^c	.18^a	.34^a	.15^a	.07
.15	-.05	.24^c	.03	.07	.06	.03	.16^b
-.29	-.23	.09	.27	-.09	-.08	-.04	.10
.13	.39^a	.02	.02	.07	.07	-.05	.16^b
.18^a	.17	.12	.16^b	.05	.13	.28^c	.24^c
.04	.08	-.08	-.09	.04	-.09	-.04	-.00
.19^c	.14	.11^c	.15^c	.14^c	.19^b	.24^c	.16^c
-.12	-.02	-.07	-.08^b	-.03	.10	.05	-.01
-.08	.00	.04	-.04	-.04	-.13	-.14^b	-.15^c
-.04	.01	-.20^c	-.08^b	-.22^c	-.05	.03	-.04^b
.56^b	.31	.27^b	.05	1.11^c	.18	.59^c	.51^c
.01	-.01	-.00	-.08^c	-.02	-.03	-.00	.01
-.04	.03	-.02	.01	-.01	.08^a	-.04	-.00
.08	-.11	-.09	.02	-.00	.17^a	-.06	.06
-.61^a	.24	-.61^c	-.58^c	-.60^c	-.43	-.08	-.25^b
241	204	602	553	499	189	500	883
26	26	26	26	26	26	26	26
214	177	575	526	472	162	473	856
.59	.49	.76	.61	.69	.56	.60	.63
.89	.80	.71	.42	.88	.98	1.06	.68
.12	-.59	.76	-.09	1.14	-.71	.98	-.27
1.05	1.03	1.05	.80	1.22	1.23	1.12	.97

(continued)

TABLE 6.3 (continued)

Coefficients of the Multilinear Regression Equation for Predicting
Faculty Salaries in Comprehensive Universities and Colleges I and II

Predictors	Field: Sex:	Biological/Physical Science	
		Men	Women
Constant		3.06	0.60
2 Date of birth		-.06	-.01
3 Marital status		.06	.23
4 No. of child.		.09	-.44
5 Highest degree		.77[c]	.59[b]
6 Year of degree		-.08	-.04
7 B.A. prestigious		-.08	.06
8 Graduate prest.		.24	-.24
9 Support		.14	-.08
11 Years academe		.04	-.10
12 Years present		-.04	.26[a]
13 Qual. present		-.26[c]	-.06
14 No. articles		.52[c]	.53[b]
15 No. books		.23[a]	.12
16 Assoc. research		.43	.72
17 No. research		-.20[a]	.18
18 No. consulting		.19	-.16
19 Research/Teach.		-.10	-.11
20 Administrative		.19[c]	.41[c]
21 Consulting		-.03	-.14
22 Prof. practice		-.04	-.03
23 Hours taught		-.08[a]	-.10
24 Salary base		.92[c]	.82[b]
27 Birth x no. art.		-.07[c]	-.05
29 Birth x no. child.		.00	.08
30 Sex x mar. x age		-.09	-.02
31 Part-time		.63[b]	-.65
No. observations		253	124
No. variables		26	26
Res'l. d.f.		226	97
Multiple R-squared		.75	.73
Res'l. Mean square		.70	.97
Mean opp. sex res'l.		-.01	.05
S.D. opp. sex res'l.		1.06	1.07

Education		Fine Arts		Humanities		Social Science	
Men	Women	Men	Women	Men	Women	Men	Women
5.27	1.16	4.37	2.07	5.78	2.31	5.62	1.34
-.10	.05	-.11	.11	-.02	.01	-.08	.04
.25	-.08	.16	-.52	.11	.10	.31	-.13
-.05	.26	-.11	-.23	$.57^c$	-.22	.44	-.24
$.71^c$	$.88^c$	$.79^b$	.28	$.44^c$	$.63^c$	$.64^b$	$.54^b$
$-.14^b$	-.02	-.06	-.04	$-.14^b$	-.02	-.14	-.02
.41	.30	.39	.31	.07	$.29^a$	.01	-.02
-.18	.11	.22	-.11	.01	-.03	$.47^a$	.23
.08	.02	-.06	.07	$.24^b$	.02	-.03	.01
.13	$.14^b$	.20	$.23^b$	.04	.10	-.03	.14
-.08	.03	-.04	.01	$.12^a$	$.14^b$	-.03	.10
$-.16^b$	$-.16^c$	$-.23^b$	-.07	$-.11^a$	$-.09^a$	$-.25^c$	$-.16^b$
.15	$.40^b$	.03	.19	.05	$.33^c$	-.08	$.77^c$
.18	$.31^b$	.25	$.68^c$	$.37^c$	.14	$.43^b$	.12
-.33	-.07	-.33	-.17	-.09	-.24	-.16	.06
.06	-.18	.16	$.68^c$	-.16	-.07	.07	.16
.14	.09	.03	.21	.13	-.01	.14	-.01
.05	-.07	-.01	.10	-.04	-.03	-.03	-.03
$.11^a$	$.07^a$	$.27^c$	-.08	.00	$.13^b$	$.17^a$	$.26^c$
-.03	-.01	-.07	-.12	$-.18^a$	.03	.06	-.07
-.15	-.10	-.02	-.09	-.04	-.10	-.12	-.08
-.08	-.04	.06	-.07	$-.26^c$	$-.12^a$	$-.19^a$	-.04
$.58^c$	$.59^c$	-.20	$.57^b$	.14	$.43^c$	.37	.23
-.01	$-.06^a$	.01	-.03	-.00	$-.06^b$	.02	$-.11^c$
.02	-.07	.04	.02	$-.08^b$	.04	-.07	.05
-.01	.03	-.16	$.16^a$	-.01	.00	.06	.01
-.21	$-.40^a$	-.43	$-.94^c$	$-.65^b$	$-.59^b$	-.31	-.38
194	303	123	153	238	347	177	139
26	26	26	26	26	26	26	26
167	276	96	126	211	320	150	112
.67	.66	.64	.68	.70	.68	.67	.78
.90	.73	1.01	.60	.77	.62	1.07	.68
.55	-.15	.90	.17	.27	-.18	.40	-.37
.99	.96	1.22	1.00	1.03	.97	1.25	1.08

(continued)

TABLE 6.3 (continued)

Coefficients of the Multilinear Regression Equation for Predicting
Faculty Salaries in Liberal Arts Colleges I

Predictors	Field: Sex:	Biological–Physical Science	
		Men	Women
Constant		$-.30$	0.95
2 Date of birth		$-.14$	$.00$
3 Marital status		$.21$	$-.08$
4 No. of child.		$-.08$	$.01$
5 Highest degree		$.26$	$.70^b$
6 Year of degree		$.21^c$	$.04$
7 B.A. prestigious		$-.00$	$-.30$
8 Graduate prest.		$-.04$	$-.06$
9 Support		$.16$	$.12$
11 Years academe		$.34^c$	$.10$
12 Years present		$.01$	$.21^a$
13 Qual. present		$-.31^b$	$-.19$
14 No. articles		$.54^c$	$.06$
15 No. books		$.04$	$.60^b$
16 Assoc. research		$-.43$	$-.48$
17 No. research		$-.01$	$-.10$
18 No. consulting		$.27^a$	$.74^c$
19 Research/Teach.		$-.07$	$.13$
20 Administrative		$.08$	$.26^b$
21 Consulting		$.08$	$-.07$
22 Prof. practice		$.19$	$-.36^a$
23 Hours taught		$-.12^b$	$.02$
24 Salary base		$.48^a$	$-.43^a$
27 Birth x no. art.		$-.06^b$	$-.01$
29 Birth x no. child.		$.01$	$-.03$
30 Sex x mar. x age		$.11$	$.05$
31 Part-time		$-.22$	$-.41$
No. observations		156	140
No. variables		26	26
Res'l. d.f.		129	113
Multiple R-squared		$.78$	$.76$
Res'l. mean square		$.52$	$.73$
Mean opp. sex res'l.		$.59$	$-.61$
S.D. opp. sex res'l.		1.04	1.16

Education		Fine Arts		Humanities		Social Science	
Men	Women	Men	Women	Men	Women	Men	Women
2.74	1.00	3.10	3.09	5.99	4.71	2.23	4.00
-.48	-.02	-.09	-.08	.02	-.06	.04	-.1-
1.49	-.03	-.37	-.20	.52	-.01	.51	-.62
.11	-.19	.21	-.28	.51^c	.20	.03	-.63
-.18	.35^a	.12	.05	.36^b	.36^c	.13	.12
.17	-.02	-.00	.05	-.22^c	-.05	-.10	.08
1.35^a	.65^b	.70	.34	.07	-.06	-.07	.12
.24	.13	.37	.16	.22	-.09	.09	.13
.28	.22^a	.12	.01	-.04	.12	.01	.21
.14	.17^a	.07	.09	.10	.22^c	.31^a	.04
-.02	-.12	.21	.04	.09	-.00	-.20	-.01
-.27	-.01	.11	-.19	-.33^c	-.31^c	-.26	-.26
-.37	.26	.45	.19	.08	.26^b	.34	.36
-.28	-.13	.46^a	.07	.27^b	.04	.35^a	.38
-.98	.56	-.91	.54	-.38	-.36	.11	-.18
1.04	-.23	.45^a	-.06	-.02	.05	.20	-.00
-.46	.16	-.10	.18	.12	.36	-.01	.18
-.01	.21	.15	-.06	-.10	.06	.28	.04
-.09	.24^c	-.10	.23^a	.20^c	.21^c	.29^b	.18
.31	-.04	.09	-.10	-.06	-.12^a	.01	-.08
-.34	.00	.28	-.01	-.09	-.01	-.17	.11
-.15	-.10^a	-.24^b	-.12	-.05	-.06	-.09	-.07
1.17^a	-.15	-.59	-.22	.21	.19^a	.12	-.53^a
.13	-.01	-.08	.01	-.00	-.03^a	-.03	-.05
-.04	.02	-.06	.01	-.07^b	-.03	.03	.09
.03	.04	.26	.05	-.07	-.11^a	-.04	.09
-.15	-.76^b	-.02	-.86^a	-.11	-.64^c	-.45	-.72^b
47	108	54	93	221	292	127	81
26	26	26	26	26	26	26	26
20	81	27	66	194	265	100	54
.83	.76	.85	.70	.79	.72	.60	.78
.80	.38	.57	.64	.62	.56	1.09	.36
.75	-.36	.70	-1.38	.09	.06	1.14	-.11
1.21	1.56	1.13	1.30	.89	.95	1.25	.85

(continued)

TABLE 6.3 (continued)

Coefficients of the Multilinear Regression Equation for Predicting
Faculty Salaries in Liberal Arts Colleges II and Two-Year Colleges

Predictors	Sex:	Biological/Phy-sical Science		Education	
Field:		Men	Women	Men	Women
Constant		-2.17	.94	2.18	-.12
2 Date of birth		-.04	.00	.13	.01
3 Marital status		.04	.08	.52	.02
4 No. of child.		.24	.99^c	.27	.06
5 Highest degree		.35	.30	.50	.02
6 Year of degree		.07	-.00	-.08	-.02
7 B.A. prestigious		.22	.59	.09	.53^a
8 Graduate prest.		.19	-.14	-.17	-.04
9 Support		.04	-.17	-.08	.27^a
11 Years academe		.26^c	.14	.29^a	.11
12 Years present		-.02	-.07	-.22	-.01
13 Qual. present		.20^a	.07	.17	.46^c
14 No. articles		-.09	.36	-.10	.10
15 No. books		.09	-.36	.43^a	-.14
16 Assoc. research		.05	-.18	-.23	-.48
17 No. research		-.06	-.07	-.61	-.21
18 No. consulting		.09	.75^b	.20	.11
19 Research/Teach.		.15	-.07	-.15	.16
20 Administrative		.19^c	.12	-.08	.02
21 Consulting		-.15	-.09	-.12	-.09
22 Prof. practice		-.21^b	-.31^a	-.02	-.14^a
23 Hours taught		-.03	.06	-.03	-.04
24 Salary base		.18	.04	.44	.08
27 Birth x no. art.		.04	-.01	.01	.03
29 Birth x no. child.		-.02	-.16^b	-.05	-.06
30 Sex x mar. x age		.10	-.07	-.04	.05
31 Part-time		-.11	-.06	-.69	-.13
No. observations		250	180	88	207
No. variables		26	26	26	26
Res'l. d.f.		223	153	61	180
Multiple R-squared		.48	.35	.51	.32
Res'l. mean square		.79	1.04	.95	.96
Mean opp. sex res'l.		.10	-.53	.96	-.23
S.D. opp. sex res'l.		1.14	1.17	1.11	1.21

Fine Arts		Humanities		Social Science		New Professions	
Men	Women	Men	Women	Men	Women	Men	Women
-2.31	.13	-3.03	-.93	2.36	-2.90	5.75	-1.85
-.01	.15[b]	.13	.05	-.00	-.05	.12	-.04
-.42	-.40	-.06	-.12	-.02	.13	-1.28	-.01
.51	-.22	.50[b]	.13	-.12	.01	.48	-.16
.78[a]	.54[b]	.37[b]	.39[c]	.59[a]	.11	1.08[b]	.31[a]
.07	-.04	-.01	-.01	-.15	.17[a]	-.11	.02
-.49	.08	.17	.39[b]	-.19	-.15	-.29	.44[a]
.07	-.22	.31	.20[a]	-.29	.13	-1.00	.01
-.02	-.12	.01	.14[a]	.39[a]	.09	-.29	.13
.06	.11	.18[a]	.14[b]	.24	.19	.14	-.01
.12	.13	.08	.05	-.05	.07	-.08	.11
.50[a]	.01	.25[a]	.20[c]	.39[b]	.26	-.45	.54[b]
-.28	.31	.03	.10	.45	.05	1.67	-.02
.00	.09	.29[a]	.09	-.07	-.02	-.47	.09
-.42	-.18	.51	.21	-.62	.46	1.10	-.20
.62	.08	.20	-.00	-.08	.75[b]	.13	.58[a]
-.17	-.07	.15	.17	.12	.17	.16	-.19
.14	.18	.11	.09	.06	.03	-.12	-.13
.17	.12	.13[a]	.08[a]	.23[a]	.07	.06	.14[b]
-.13	-.08	.05	-.05	-.21	.03	-.61	-.05
-.10	-.02	-.12	-.06	.00	-.24[a]	-.26	-.07
-.11	-.04	-.03	-.02	-.06	-.20[a]	.03	.00
.43	.04	-.05	-.03	.46	.06	.67	.22
.10	-.08	.00	-.01	-.08	.02	-.20	.02
-.05	.03	-.08[a]	-.03	.02	-.05	-.04	-.01
.09	.16[a]	.11	.04	.04	.11	.12	.12
-.23	-.19	-.51[a]	-.51[b]	-.37	-.58	-.71	-.14
93	139	241	469	112	124	47	223
26	26	26	26	26	26	26	26
66	112	214	442	85	97	20	196
.43	.48	.46	.38	.63	.48	.75	.41
1.19	.59	.95	.73	1.16	1.13	1.22	.75
1.26	-.81	.57	-.61	.97	-.73	1.06	-1.18
1.15	.95	.98	.91	1.29	1.32	1.55	1.61

[a] Individual coefficient differs from zero at 0.05 significance level (two-sided).

[b] Differs at 0.01 level.

[c] Differs at 0.001 level.

Source: Martin A. Trow, "Appendix—Carnegie Commission on Higher Education National Survey of Faculty and Student Opinion," in Martin A. Trow, ed., Teachers and Students (New York: McGraw-Hill, 1975).

are of interest, as are the relative coefficients of the important predictor variables, but they are not of principal concern in developing
measures of equal opportunities for women.

We want to ask what salary a man would receive if he were paid
not by the men's equation, but by the women's equation, and how this
compares with his actual salary. We find that in the great majority
of cases, men appear to be overpaid when their actual salary is compared with the salary predicted by the women's equation; the residual
difference tends to be positive by about $3,000 and often by as much
as $5,000 or $7,000. Correspondingly, when a woman's salary is
compared with the estimate, from the men's equation, of the salary
of a man with the same characteristics except for sex, she tends to
be underpaid by $3,000, $5,000, or even $7,000. The distribution of
these residuals is shown in Figure 6.4. The shift in distribution is
evident in every type-field category, but it is particularly striking in
the selective universities and in the sciences, just where salaries
tend to be higher and women scarcer. The next-to-last line in Table
6.3 gives the mean residual from the opposite-sex equation (the mean
overpayment) for men and for women. Notice that this figure tends
to be positive (overpayment) for men and negative (underpayment)
for women, almost without exception, and by about one salary interval (about $3,000).

The mean residual from the opposite sex equation should be zero
if there are equal rewards for men and women (as occurs with the
mean residual from the own-sex equation). Admittedly, the determination of salary is complex and the results presented are statistical. Nevertheless, the differences found are entirely too large to
be due to chance and appear to reflect discrimination. Further, as
Astin and Bayer pointed out, insofar as there is discrimination in
the predictor variables (for example, the difficulties experienced by
women in being admitted to graduate school to obtain the doctorate
and in entering the faculty at all), we are underestimating the bias in
salaries for women.

How can these computations be used to obtain equal salary opportunities for women faculty in particular universities and colleges?
The simplest procedure would be to increase the salaries of all women in each type-field category by the amount of the mean opposite-
sex residual in the appropriate column of Table 6.3. For example,
for the statistics department of the University of California, Berkeley,
we would look in Table 6.3 under biological and physical sciences
and read -1.04 salary intervals as the mean underpayment. Thus, to
compensate for bias the salary of each woman should be increased
by 1.04 salary interval, that is, by about $3,000.

With a little effort, each institution could compute the residual
difference between actual salary and that predicted from Table 6.3

for each member of its faculty, using the appropriate columns in Table 6.3 for the opposite sex. Each institution can thus compute its mean residuals (overpayment of men and underpayment of women) rather than using the average of similar institutions. Our computations show that the results will not be very different.

It is instructive to note which coefficients are different for men and women. The most striking difference occurs in predictor no. 11, the number of years in academe. The coefficient is always larger, often twice as large, for men as for women, which means simply that the increase in salary over the years is at a correspondingly faster rate for men than for women. This coefficient, and others, indicate that women who have been in academe for a longer time are even more discriminated against than newcomers. Actually, detailed studies of the residuals, such as those shown in Figure 6.4, indicate that there is a general shift of about $1,500 to $2,000 toward underpayment of women combined with a lack of exceptionally high payments to women. With some refinement the coefficients presented in Table 6.3 provide a means for obtaining more equal salaries for women and men of the same ability and performance.

The comparisons with Table 6.3 suggested above can also be used to examine possible underpayment of minority faculty. We have done this with the Carnegie Commission survey data. We find that black women are underpaid when compared with all men, and black men are overpaid when compared with all women. Also, Oriental women are underpaid when compared with all men, and Oriental men are overpaid when compared with all women. Somewhat surprisingly, the mean underpayment of black women and of Oriental women is not significantly different from the mean underpayment of white women (actually it is a little less), and the mean overpayment of black men and of Oriental men is not significantly different from that of white men (actually it is a little less). The difference between the sexes is maintained but, rather surprisingly, there appear no significant differences among races. Again, we must remember that the Carnegie Commission survey is retrospective and must give only a bound, since we have no information on qualified minority members who are not employed nor on discrimination in the predictor variables. Further study is required.

SEX DIFFERENCES IN INTELLECTUAL ABILITY

Opportunities in higher education depend on intellectual ability. It has been said that the decreasing percentage of women at each higher level of academe is a reflection of the scarcity of women of outstanding ability. The usual measures of composite intellectual

FIGURE 6.4

Amount of Overpayment or Underpayment: Distribution of the Difference Between Actual and Predicted Salary, Estimated from the Multilinear Equation for Opposite Sex, for Male and Female Faculty Members

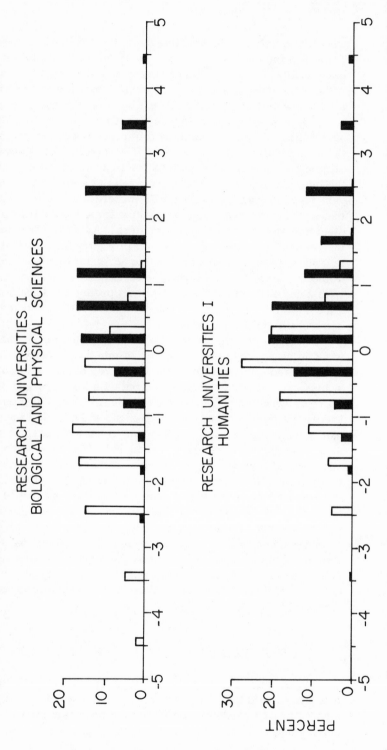

RESEARCH UNIVERSITIES I
BIOLOGICAL AND PHYSICAL SCIENCES

RESEARCH UNIVERSITIES I
HUMANITIES

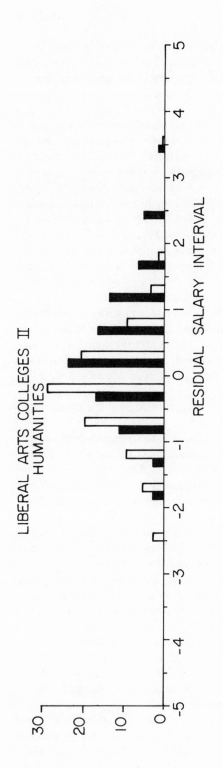

LIBERAL ARTS COLLEGES II
HUMANITIES

RESIDUAL SALARY INTERVAL

Women

Men

Notes: Overpayment is positive; underpayment is negative.
One salary interval is about $3,000.

Source: Martin A. Trow, "Appendix—Carnegie Commission on Higher Education National Survey of Faculty and Student Opinion," in Martin A. Trow, ed., Teachers and Students (New York: McGraw-Hill, 1975).

ability, such as IQ tests, do not answer this question because they are constructed (not always successfully) to balance sex differences by adding or deleting items at which boys or girls excel. On the other hand, the component subtests in the college admission examination and in higher-level admission tests (such as Graduate Record, Medical School Aptitude, and Law School Aptitude) have been sex-balanced on the verbal aptitude tests but no effort has been made to balance the component measures of quantitative ability. A comprehensive study should be made to estimate how much of the lag in quantitative scores is due to differences in training, to lapse of time since studying mathematics, and so forth, and how much is unexplained. Since women perform better, on the average, after admission even when sorted by their admission scores (see Figure 6.5 for an example), the evidence is that the tests are not fair predictors of future academic performance. They require revision to achieve better sex balance. With the present tests the cutoff point in score should be about 10 percent lower for women than for men.

Other tests of quantitative ability indicate sex differences that are not consistent. One of the more recent studies, the large international study by T. Husen comparing 12 countries, found a sex difference in achievement of less than one-fifth of the standard deviation of the scores of boys or of girls alone. This was combined with markedly less interest and training in mathematics for girls.[2] The National Assessment of Educational Progress in Science found differences in the number of correct answers of 3 percent more for males at age 17 and of 10 percent more for young adult males, both only a fraction of the standard deviation of males.[3] At all ages the differences lie chiefly within the physical sciences; males tend to outperform on exercises such as the one concerning a block sliding down an inclined plane, and females do better on the questions regarding human reproduction.

There is extensive and continuing evidence of sex differences in visual spatial ability (embedded figures test or rod and frame test), starting in the teens and increasing through high school, with boys' scores exceeding girls', on the average, by about .50 standard deviation. It is not known how much of this lag is due to differences in training and experience, although there is speculation. The visual spatial difference has been relabeled and overgeneralized, on the basis of very little or no evidence, as indicative of global (female) versus analytical (male) cognitive style. As J. A. Sherman points out, the fallacy involved is similar to the conclusion, based on findings of superior female ability to decontextualize the red and green figures on the Ishara color blindness test, that women are more analytical than men.[4] The relationship, if any, between performing well on an embedded figures test and/or on a color blindness test and performing well on, say, a mathematical achievement test is not known.

FIGURE 6.5

Comparison of Grade–Point Average and American College Testing
Total Score of Men and Women

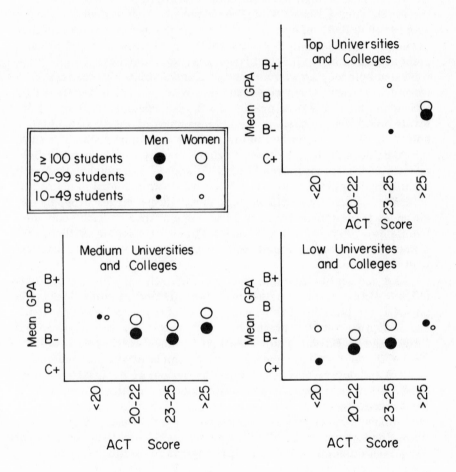

Source: Martin A. Trow, "Appendix—Carnegie Commission on
Higher Education National Survey of Faculty and Student Opinion," in
Martin A. Trow, ed., Teachers and Students (New York: McGraw-
Hill, 1975.

When we consider ability at the faculty level, we are not much
concerned with the general population or with the entrants to graduate
or professional school. We need to consider the ability of the pool
from which faculty are selected, largely the holders of doctorates.
L. R. Harmon studied the intellectual ability of those who received
the Ph.D. during 1959-62—35,190 people who had graduated from
about 10,000 U.S. high schools. Through the use of a representative
sample of the classmates of each Ph.D., data on high school grade
point averages in English and languages, social sciences, mathematics, and science, as well as rank in class and intelligence test scores
were converted to standard scores (mean 50, standard deviation 10).
Harmon's purpose was to predict the field of specialization of the doctorate holder on the basis of the six measures of ability at the high
school level. A by-product of his study is his comparison of the doctorate holders by sex, by type of school, and by field. In every field,
on each of the six measures of ability, women score higher than men.
Women who married before receiving the doctorate tend to score the
highest, followed by single women, then, after a bigger drop, by single men, then by married men. The comparisons on each score for
two fields are shown in Figure 6.6. For one reason or another, the
women who manage to complete the doctorate are more able than the
men who do so.[5]

But one could argue that ability in high school, although correla-
ted with ability as an assistant professor, is not the same thing. The
payoff at the later level is on papers published, on fellowships won,
and so forth. But here again women are ahead, R. J. Simon, S. M.
Clark, and K. Galway studied the 1,764 women who had received
the Ph.D. between 1958 and 1962 and a sample of 492 men matched
on field and degree date. The full-time academic professionals were
compared in each field. Women were much more likely to have at
least one postdoctoral fellowship, they published as much as men (married women without children somewhat more than men, unmarried
women and women with children slightly less). Yet these women were
much less often employed in the prestigious institutions that provide
the pressures, stimulation, and lower teaching loads that aid publication rates.[6]

Other criticisms, such as "She'll only get married and quit" also
prove to be myths. Studies at individual universities find that the attrition rate is lower for women faculty than for men. The 1973 faculty survey by the American Council on Education found that women
faculty were less likely to have interrupted their professional careers
for more than one year for military or family reasons.

On all counts women appear to more than deserve equal opportunities in academe. The measures we have described here can be used
to check whether or not they are receiving equal opportunities for em-

FIGURE 6.6

Comparison of High School Ability of Doctorate Holders,
by Sex and Marital Status

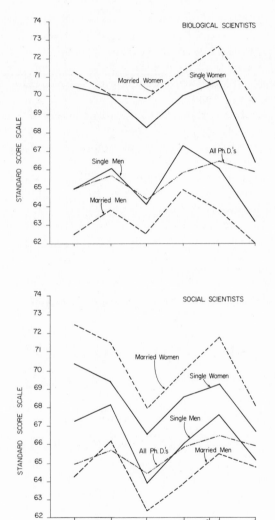

Source: L. R. Harmon, "High School Ability Patterns—A Backward Look from the Doctorate," Scientific Manpower Report, no. 6
(Washington, D.C.: Office Scientific Personnel, National Academy
of Sciences, August 20, 1965).

ployment and in salary. They can also be used to monitor admission rates for women students.

NOTES

1. H. S. Astin and A. E. Bayer, "Sex Discrimination in Academe," Educational Record 53 (1972): 101-18.

2. T. Husen, ed., International Study of Achievement in Mathematics, 2 vols. (Stockholm: Almquist & Wiksell, 1967; New York: John Wiley & Sons, 1967).

3. National Assessment of Educational Progress, National Assessment Report 4, 1969-70, Science: Group Results for Sex, Region, and Size of Community (Washington, D.C.: Education Commission of the States, 1971).

4. J. A. Sherman, "Problem of Sex Differences in Space Perception and Aspects of Intellectual Functioning," Psychological Review 74, no. 4 (1967): 290-99.

5. L. R. Harmon, "High School Ability Patterns—A Backward Look from the Doctorate," Scientific Manpower Report, no. 6 (Washington, D.C.: Office of Scientific Personnel, National Academy of Sciences, August 20, 1965).

6. R. J. Simon, S. M. Clark, and K. Galway, "The Woman Ph.D.: A Recent Profile," Social Problems 15 (1967): 221-36.

7

It is important at this time to discuss the issue of the growth of women in science in pragmatic terms. This discussion will have a practical and constructive focus because I believe that this is a very pivotal and precious moment for women in academia that must not be lost. We still face problems, but suddenly there are a good many things going for us. Attitudes change slowly, but it is now widely recognized that women have not had a fair chance. Considerable effort is being made to rectify the situation. It behooves women in academia, without letting up the pressures for affirmative action, to concentrate their major efforts on building commendable and, if possible, impressive records of professional achievement. Otherwise, the judgment could be made that women have been given a chance and that nothing has come of it. It is essential to have evidence of women's productivity, as well as of past discrimination against them, to keep the doors of opportunity open.

Although the problem of bias against women in academia is not restricted to the field of science, I believe that women scientists have a special responsibility when it comes to demonstrating productivity. Science is to the humanities and the social sciences as track and baseball are to the creative arts: the ground rules are clearer. Subjective judgments still enter the picture, especially at the lower levels; but outstanding performance is not easily denied. If one has good training and a chance to compete, talent can make its mark. Furthermore, the relative measurability of scientific achievement is a primary reason that so many students, both men and women, shift out of the sciences during their undergraduate years. It is not that they are doing badly in their courses but that they can, by simple comparison, determine how much more capable a few of their classmates are. It is true that "big science," with its research teams,

115

may sometimes make it more difficult to assess the contributions of individuals; but in comparison with other disciplines, the sciences still make relatively favorable proving grounds.

The sciences offer a special challenge to women as well as an opportunity to demonstrate their productivity. It seems to be culturally accepted that women have relatively little aptitude for science. Therefore, achievements of those in the field will carry more weight. Statistically speaking, at this point in history the record is not strong; but this is no reason for discouraging those who do have high ability or for refusing to see that there may be problems. Only a very few of the applicants to Radcliffe have math aptitude scores above the median of the scores of the men who apply to Harvard, but a higher proportion of the entering women think they will major in mathematics. Are these lower math aptitude scores a unique outcome of the female socialization experience? What accounts for the higher proportion of women intending to concentrate in math? How meaningful are the differences between these aptitude scores? Can women's aptitude for math and the attitudes to which it gives rise be overcome or compensated for? Regardless of the answer to these questions, I believe that the careers of those women who have chosen science need to be supported. What are some of the practical things that can be done?

RECRUITING SCIENCE STUDENTS

The first area to concentrate on is undergraduate admissions. Few individuals of either sex enter the sciences after freshman year; the flow is in the other direction. Potentially able young women scientists need to be identified and encouraged as they graduate from high school. Unfortunately, neither school counselors nor college admissions committees are apt to see the potentialities in some of the relatively nonverbal, socially immature, and rather stubborn "science freaks." Worse yet, they do not like them. These students can benefit greatly from career counseling, and a half hour's conversation with a candidate in a laboratory can be very revealing for both sides. While the specific procedural details may vary, any signals that can be given to admissions personnel, and encouragement given to youngsters, no matter at which institution they eventually study, will not be a waste of time.

Even at the graduate level, the selection of women often is influenced too much by their scores and college grades and too little by an assessment of their originality and motivation. This is true in many fields, not just in the sciences. Faculty tend to give more thought to how different women will fit into the laboratory or the department than to whether one of them might have a real spark of genius. Again, those who care can help. If the right young women can get top-notch training in the sciences, the chances of demonstrating high productivity later will be greatly increased. The selection of graduate women in many fields could be done more imaginatively, more seriously, more effectively than is now the case.

FACULTY ATTITUDES

Admissions, however, probably is less important than the attitudes and expectations of faculty and students in the department. The ironic thing about the higher education of women is that the further they progress, the less their accomplishments are valued. The family that is desperately eager to get a daughter into a prestigious college may have very little interest in whether she completes her doctorate. And faculty members sometimes overlook lapses that they would not tolerate in a male graduate student. Subtle complications enter the picture in those institutions where there is an assumption that most male students are future leaders. The women are known to be bright but are not thought to be important, not expected to make outstanding contributions. The very different expectations for women students may be more evident in such institutions than elsewhere, affecting their self-images adversely and negating other favorable influences.

Faculty women, as their numbers increase and their concerns broaden, undoubtedly can give a great deal more support to younger colleagues than they have in the past. Not only do students need to see believable models, but they also need to feel that they are seen by those models and that their potentialities are valued. It is generally known how influential parental support can be, even when parents have not themselves had the benefit of much education. Even if a woman's own scientific attainments are modest, she can give consistent and demanding support to promising younger women. This continuing encouragement and support of potential women scientists may have more influence on them and on males in academia than any other method.

INSTITUTIONAL FLEXIBILITY

Given the pattern of most women's lives, another practical step that can be taken is to keep the doors of opportunity open to those women of ability and high motivation who live within reach of academic institutions. Continuity is very important: If a young wife wishes to do graduate work and has the ability to do so, every effort should be made to give her the opportunity. If she has completed her doctorate but needs the chance to pursue her research and demonstrate her productivity as a scientist, this should be made possible. For far too many women, lack of a chance to demonstrate their research capability has been the final bottleneck to a recognized professional career. Our experience at the Radcliffe Institute has shown how much difference just a little help can make at this critical time. Over the past 10 years we have given small grants and other assistance, never for more than two years, to some 200 artists, scholars, and scientists, so that they can pursue independent projects of their own devising and publish their results (the chance to publish their own work is vitally important). Former Institute fellows, some of whom never contemplated academic careers, are now teaching or holding good administrative jobs in 55 different colleges and universities. Although assistance to these women may result in limiting the availability of funds for beginning graduate students, it can be an important factor in bringing to fruition careers that have been interrupted or stalled.

During the childbearing and child-raising period, flexibility in scheduling will be essential for many women; this flexibility should be viewed as part of academic freedom. Faculties pride themselves on knowing quality and honoring it in spite of all sorts of eccentricities, believing that in the end such a policy will be productive. It is only because their expectations of women have been so trivial that they have shown such rigidity with respect to part-time scheduling. I am well aware of the need to reexamine the basic patterns imposed on women's lives and see this beginning to happen, but I do not consider it a valid reason for retaining rigidities that are impeding the career development of many able women.

In this connection, pressure should be exerted on the federal government, the American Association of University Women, and other fellowship-granting groups to liberalize their programs and prorate fellowships in cases where the grantee has valid reasons for wishing to study or work on a part-time schedule. Ability and promise should be the criteria of selection, not "effort reporting." The only exception I know to the federal government's requirement that fellowship holders be full-time is the trainee program of the National Science Foundation. It took five years of needling as a member of the National Science Board to achieve that change in policy, and I suspect that it was possible only because traineeships are going out of existence. I believe that only one university, the University of Washington, has taken advantage of the new provisions. All five of the women to whom they have given part-time traineeships have done well and, within or after one year, have been able to make suitable arrangements at home to shift to a full-time basis. It often is during the first year of graduate work, or of resuming graduate studies after the birth of a child, that women most need to work part-time; but it is precisely at that point that institutions have been most rigid.

Finally, each university should have an up-to-date list of the women to whom it has awarded advanced degrees, with information about their subsequent careers and current status. This information is necessary in order to respond to inquiries from other institutions seeking qualified women. It also is needed for self-evaluation. How well were they selected, trained, and assisted later in their careers? What can be done for them at this point? It is hoped that each academic department will make its own study, and each administration show an interest in findings and proposed plans. The interest of top management does make a difference. So does the approval of the rank and file. Let us not neglect to show our appreciation of the steps that our male colleagues are now taking, slow as they may have been to do so. Far more important than what has happened in the past is what will happen in the future, and we need their cooperation.

8

SEX DISCRIMINATION
AT UNIVERSITIES:
AN OMBUDSMAN'S VIEW
Alice H. Cook

In the fall of 1969 I became Cornell's first university ombudsman, a position I held for two years. My major task was to hear
"complaints from anyone in the University . . . about anyone in
authority in the University or about the operation of the University."
The office became for me an intensive seminar in problems of university structure and functioning. I shall focus here specifically on the
problems of women, and mainly of professional women as I became
familiar with them in my term of office as ombudsman.

Although Cornell is an old and proud member of the Ivy League,
it has had women students and a few women faculty members from
its very early years. The problems it now faces are neither new
nor newly generated. I have been impressed, as I have read the
rapidly growing library of studies on women in higher education,
how very much alike we all are. For that reason I dare to think that
the Cornell experience is not so special or peculiar that it may not
feed the mainstream of current literature, bearing corroboration of
larger trends and adding velocity and direction to its many currents.

Let me briefly sketch what I see the general circumstances of
women in higher education to be. You may safely assume that the
Cornell experience beds neatly into this frame. Among the various
colleges within a university, women students are distributed very un-

---

This chapter was originally presented at the 138th annual meet-
ing of the American Association for the Advancement of Science sym-
posium "Women in Academia." It was subsequently published as
"Sex Discrimination at Universities: An Ombudsman's View" in
American Association of University Professors Bulletin 58, no. 3
(September 1972), and is reprinted with permission.

evenly, with relatively high proportions of enrollment in the colleges
of arts, home economics, social sciences, and, where they exist,
in professional schools of library science, education, nursing, and
social work. They are represented only exceptionally in colleges of
law, veterinary medicine, architecture, and engineering. They represent a minority, sometimes very small, in agriculture and medicine. Among faculty a comparable picture emerges, but only very
rarely does the proportion of female to male faculty correspond
favorably to the proportions of female to male students. A 1971
study at Cornell shows, for example, that although 28 percent of the
students in the College of Arts and Sciences are women, only 5.2 percent of the faculty are women; that in the College of Human Ecology,
where more than 90 percent of the students are women, only 58 percent of the faculty are women. Moreover, while total faculty composition shows that only 7.5 percent are women, even these are heavily
grouped on the lower rungs of the academic ladder. Of the 1,432
members of the faculty on the Ithaca campus, 108 are women; of
these 108, 22 are full professors (12 in the College of Human Ecology),
as compared with 658 men; 47 are associate professors (25 in the College of Human Ecology), as compared with 317 men; and 42 are assistant professors (16 in the College of Human Ecology), as compared
with 349 men. These numbers represent a slight favorable shift over
the past year. Two more women are assistant professors than was
the case a year ago.[1] Similarly, though at a somewhat more satis-
factory pace, quotas on the acceptance of women students are disap-
pearing and their active recruitment is now a matter of policy in the
College of Engineering and the Law School.[2]

    Since this article was first written, Cornell University has created
an Office of Affirmative Action whose director is responsible for
drafting and enforcing affirmative action programs for women, blacks,
and other minorities. It is the author's expectation that many of the
specific inequities noted here will shortly be the object of remedial
measures.

    On the administrative side, however, no college dean is a woman;
perhaps a half dozen departments on the campus have women chairmen; the highest positions that women hold in the administration are
those of associate dean of students and associate personnel director.
In the individual colleges, several women hold posts as assistant director of admissions, but only in Human Ecology is the director a woman. On the board of trustees, six of fifty are women; but, of these,
two are elected by alumni, two by students, and one by the University
Senate.

    In the parafaculty positions, the picture is markedly different.
Of 469 academic positions at the ranks of lecturer and research associate, 142, or 30 percent, are held by women.[3] If one considers the

numbers at the lowest range of the academic progression, instructors,
we must add 28 men and 23 women—approximately an equal division
of the sexes at this location—and we arrive at a female employment of
33 percent with rank below that of assistant professor.

Although I do not have figures available, my strong impression
is that the number of women in nonacademic supervisory positions is
very small indeed, even in housekeeping departments. In the libraries the top posts are all occupied by men, although women are head
librarians in six of the departmental or college libraries.

This situation is not propitious; it likewise is not unusual. In
view of these circumstances, it would be strange indeed if allegations
of sex discrimination had not come to the ombudsman's office. What
were they?

BARRIERS CONFRONTING WOMEN

The first group illustrated the difficulties of young married women in finding academic posts. Ithaca, not unlike many universities,
is, as we say, splendidly isolated. If one wants academic employment, there is no wide range of alternatives, such as any of the larger cities these days offers. Most of these young women have accompanied their husbands to a new location. The husband typically has
the professorial appointment, albeit as an assistant, and hence is in
no position to bargain his wife into the departmental roster, much
less into an unknown other department or college. Her best offer,
if she is lucky enough to find any employment, may well be a lecture-
ship. If she has small children, she may even welcome the circumstance that makes no demands on her for research, publication, or
administrative duties. But she is in fact in an academic limbo without security and without prospects, on a year-to-year contract, for
the most part invisible to search committees looking at candidates to
fill professorial vacancies.

A second group of cases concerned those wanting to move from
limbo to the ladder. A departmental lecturer is rarely approached,
even less rarely automatically reviewed, when an opening occurs.
Instead, in my experience, she must call the attention of a search
committee chairman or a department head to her availability. In
some cases she does so with considerable surface bravado; in most
instances with deep reluctance, because her own observations, supported by husbandly advice, have informed her that one does nothing
so gross in the university as to apply directly for a position. Instead
one waits to have one's name put forward by one's graduate professor
when he receives the letter that reads, "We are looking for a bright
young man. . . ." The price of self-nomination can be high. One

young lecturer was told the search committee would first look over outsiders, since the department preferred "new blood" and someone with a "serious interest in a career." The inference she drew was that a lecturer, particularly a woman, was perceived as a dilettante or as someone perforce inadequately prepared. Another such candidate was never invited to give the standard seminar before the departmental audience, on the ground that her colleagues already knew pretty well what she was doing. Instead, two members of a four-man search committee appeared on occasion as visitors to her classroom lecture.

A third kind of problem came from women with many years of employment on what I call the parafaculty, as women who are essentially teaching assistants in large courses or supervisors of teams of such assistants, women who teach exotic languages for which demand fluctuates and is never great, women on large, funded research projects—on "soft money"—handling fieldwork or laboratory teams. A common cause of difficulty here was the lack of job definition, sometimes even the lack of a contract. If no increments were written into the grant, a woman employed on it might find herself working five or six years without an increase, while her colleagues received annual wage increases. Were such women academic employees keyed to the academic calendar with its holidays and intersessions and nine months' contracts, or were they in effect nonexempt employees working the year round with a three- or four-week vacation and the expectation that they were visibly available 39 hours a week? What was a standard number of classroom contact hours? What could happen if not enough students enrolled for a language lab? What obligation did the university have, if any, when funding ended in the middle of an academic year and reemployment, even at another institution, would not be available for months?

One can hardly blame the deans and department heads who can easily be painted in these cases as culprits. Only in exceptional cases have they set out to manipulate the market to their best advantage. The situation is more complicated, for the woman herself is heavily culpable. To be sure, as a realist she has drawn a conclusion from her assessment of her employment chances. It is that her best hope for employment lies in seeking paraprofessional and technical jobs. They allow her, moreover, to have time to manage her home and children while keeping her professional tools in use in a part-time job or a full-time one that does not include requirements for research, writing, and administration. Even when she deplores the choice she must make, she is in no position to take on the political struggle involved in changing the policy of a university of which she is not yet even a part, or of which, once employed, she is a dispensable part.

These problems of the paraprofessional are by no means confined to women, but they do fall heavily on them, in part because women make up a high proportion of the employees in these workhorse assignments. It cannot, however, be an accident that in the categories most heavily populated by women, the ordinary, minimal decencies of personnel practice are most often honored in the breach. Unquestionably women who are occupationally immobilized, as is often the case with many of these highly qualified or even overqualified women, have no bargaining power and no experience in assembling and exerting it.

A fourth category of problems related to part-time employment. Universities are among the few institutions that offer married women part-time employment. And many married women are eager to find such jobs and grateful when they are placed in them. But half-time workers often receive no fringe benefits of any kind. This makes them attractive to deans and department heads, particularly if they are under pressure to economize wherever and however they legitimately can. Moreover, the practice has been justified on the ground that because most half-time employees are women, they are probably covered by their husbands' health insurance and retirement plans. The steadily growing number of women who are heads of families through divorce, widowhood, or separation, or who have never married belies this assumption, and in any case is a negation of the principle that remuneration for the job should not be adjusted according to the personal circumstances of the jobholder.

The national statistics on earnings of professional women show not only that they receive, on an average, only 65 percent of the income of professional men but, what is more, that the gap between men's and women's earnings in this category, as in all others, is widening rather than narrowing. Probably women entering university employment today are rarely if ever receiving less than their male counterparts in comparable posts, but this was not always the case. A woman who is approaching retirement appealed to me. She came to the university for her first employment when she was widowed 15 years ago. Not only her first appointment, but also several subsequent ones, were at salaries lower than the job rating called for. Her personnel file included a letter from one supervisor who recommended to the college dean that she come on his staff at $5,600 instead of the $7,800 the job carried at that time because this amount was in line with her former earnings and because it would not be necessary to pay her, as a woman, as much as her male predecessor had received. Although those days are gone forever, the effect of them lives on. Her progression from that time forward has been reckoned on that base. She now faces retirement on a pension fixed at a proportion of her three years of highest earnings.

Such experiences point unmistakably to the determining effect of the conditions that a woman accepts as she comes into the academic marketplace. If for reasons of inexperience, necessity, or merely the fact that she takes a short-term view of her career, a woman accepts the temporary convenience of a part-time job, a paraprofessorial appointment, a piece-rate (by which I mean employment and payment by the course taught), or some other piecemeal arrangement, she is jeopardizing her lifetime opportunities and income. Until these arrangements are regularized in the light of women's special needs and circumstances, they will inevitably operate to exploit women and place them at a disadvantage.

I have not touched on two important circumstances determining the number and quality of women seeking academic positions. The first is, of course, the admissions policies of graduate schools and the kind and amount of support available to women in them as compared with men. Although graduate schools are rapidly improving, or stand ready to improve their admissions policy in favor of women, it is often still set on a quota basis: a formula that accepts the same proportion of women applicants as of men applicants. Since more men than women apply for graduate school, this can leave the actual acceptance figures in severe disproportion. Graduate schools are understandably reluctant, when support is limited, to give it to both husband and wife; but when it goes to one of a couple, it is surely more often to the man than the woman. Attrition figures that appear to show that more women fail to complete their degrees within the university's time limits than is the case with men encourage graduate school administrators to make these choices in favor of men and thus to fulfill the predicted outcome.

A coda to this consideration of the problem at the graduate school level has to do with the kind of career counseling, both formal and informal, that is available to women considering careers in college teaching or any other professional career. As is true wherever one turns in this man's world, counseling is rarely available that asks a young woman to face up realistically to planning for a multiple role as professional, mother, and wife of a professional man. Rather, she is given the requirements of the male world to which she will be expected to conform, and then she is given no help in thinking about alternative strategies in preparation for, access to, and performance on the job. She is, in effect, left to deal with the complicated problem alone, piecemeal, ad hoc.

The second circumstance is the fact that women's childbearing years, and the years that have been accepted in the male-dominated employment model as decisive for the establishment of one's career, exactly overlap. Women generally, with the exceptions of a few highly gifted ones, cannot fulfill both roles simultaneously. They

must in many cases come into the academic marketplace at a somewhat more advanced age than men; they may take more years to finish
their Ph.D.'s and, following that, to be ready for full professorial
responsibility. Yet one woman whose children are now subteens and
who got her Ph.D. at 39, two years ago, has had an agonizing difficulty in getting a position. Another who came to the university with
a degree earned at 47 was promoted to full professor and made assistant dean within five years, since her maturity and broad preacademic
experience were recognized as values to which the Ph.D. was only
the latest testimony.

INSTITUTIONAL RESPONSES

What can an ombudsman—or anyone else—do? Where do the approaches to solution of these inequities lie?

Men and women are different. This "difference" has been the
subject of toasts, not just by playboys but by scholars as well. It is
a difference, however, with which the academic world is only now beginning to deal on any but men's terms. Under these new terms,
women are treated as equals, or almost so, as long as they conform
to the conditions of employment that are convenient to men and have
been established by them. These include conformity between men and
women not only in academic preparation but also in age, in rate of
progression, in quantity of output at given stages of the progression.
If, in addition, women choose to have babies, they will be mainly
responsible for raising them and for keeping the homes in which children and father find nurture and comfort, besides doing all that their
male colleagues do in the classroom, the laboratory, the office, and
the committee room.

The radical solution that some women's groups propose is to
educate or intimidate men into sharing these family responsibilities
equally with their wives. Many academic couples are deeply committed to finding personal solutions to the problems of two careers
as well as two children. But these solutions are exceptional and personal. (Parenthetically, men who consistently try to share these
family tasks with their wives can find it as hard to carry out the
bargain as their wives find life without their assistance. A man who
moves because his wife has a better offer or whose wife becomes
full professor before he does may suffer quite as severe consequences
to his career prospects as his wife does when she assumes the secondary role.)

If we are not to insist that the academic woman remain childless
or that she carry a load so heavy that only the extraordinary person
can manage the burden, we must recognize that equality calls for
certain institutional as well as personal approaches.

Equality for women in academe, as elsewhere, calls for consideration of her unique functions. Beyond the generally accepted, standard decencies of good personnel practice at all levels of employment to which I have alluded, we must at a minimum consider the matters of maternity leave, of part-time employment at nontenured and tenured levels with appropriately extended probationary periods and intervals between tenure promotions, and of late arrival in the academic market. Not only must nepotism rules be rescinded, but we must look also at our "incest" rules. Those of our own Ph. D.'s who are unable to move into the national academic marketplace because of family ties to our own universities need to be drawn into the range of consideration for local posts, if their training and our investment in it is not to be lost to higher education.

We need to break some of the traditional hiring molds. We fling wide nets to catch the brightest young man in the field. For a while— they should not have to do it forever—search committees ought to specify that they will welcome information about bright young women as well; moreover, it will do no harm for them to indicate ways in which they will help a young woman who is head of a family meet her multiple obligations. Although under unusual circumstances deans and presidents may advertise, search committees on the whole do not. Perhaps they should. Perhaps they should add a line that applications from qualified women are welcomed.

No one, least of all women looking for an academic career, is asking that standards be lowered in order to increase the employment of women. To ask that is to impugn our whole system of higher education by suggesting that it has trained women less adequately than men or has selected them by another standard. What is called for is a concept of equity based on a special life cycle—one that, with the best will in the world, cannot and need not be compressed into a mold by and for men.

NOTES

1. Jennie Farley, "Affirmative Action for Women: Where Is It?", December 5, 1971. Mimeographed by author.

2. In 1974, 48 percent of the students and 7.9 percent of the faculty of Arts and Sciences were women; 88 percent of students and 49 percent of the faculty in the College of Human Ecology were women; the proportion of women on the faculty and para-faculty remained unchanged.

3. Derived from figures published in the Cornell Chronicle, June 3 and September 2, 1971, under the heading, "Statistics on Women Faculty and Students."

9

A CASE HISTORY OF
AFFIRMATIVE ACTION
Ruth Beach

The review of the early beginnings of affirmative action at Car-negie-Mellon University (CMU) is based in part on the paper entitled "The Report of the Commission on Women at Carnegie-Mellon University and the Problems of Its Implementation," given by Edward Schatz at the 1971 American Association for the Advancement of Science symposium.

This case history initially reviews early interest in affirmative action at CMU from 1970 through 1972, culminating in the establishment of the University Affirmative Action Office in 1973. The balance of the chapter discusses the resources, strategies, and actions of the Affirmative Action Office from 1973 to the present, concluding with some observations on the problems—both attitudinal and practical—that have been associated with its operation.

EARLY BEGINNINGS

Interest in affirmative action for CMU women began in 1970 and continued for three years before the Affirmative Action Office was established. In the middle of this period there were major changes in the leadership of the university and of the campus women's movement.

1970-71

In the fall of 1970, faculty women began to meet informally to discuss their general concerns about the status of women at CMU. Thoughts became directed toward the need for some program that would improve the status of women faculty, students, and staff. Rather than having definite problems or procedures in mind, the feeling was that someone should make a start; accordingly, a group of women began meeting on a regular basis. This group quickly expanded, took the name "Carnegie-Mellon University Academic Women," and organized itself into committees.

One of these committees (which consisted of tenured and non-tenured faculty, women staff, and students) arranged a series of meetings with the university administration, during which they requested that the university establish and fund an office to equalize the status of women at CMU. In essence, the CMU administration replied that since there was no demonstrated evidence of the unequal status of women, the specific areas and extent of any inequality would have to be investigated and identified before any action could be taken. The result of this counterproposal was the creation, in February 1971, of the Investigatory Commission on the Status and Needs of Women at Carnegie-Mellon University.

The 12 members of the commission, four men and eight women, were proposed by the women's group and appointed by the president; they included one academic dean, two vice-presidents, one male and three female faculty members, two students, two staff women, and an alumna. The president provided office space, a small operating budget, and released time from teaching to devote to commission activities. Most important, the group was charged to investigate all aspects of university operations that affected women. Specifically, the commission was charged to do the following:

1. Examine all areas of university operations as they pertained to the general problem of the status of women students, including admissions, placement services, housing, classroom treatment, and educational counseling; of women faculty and staff, including employment, retention, promotion, and salaries; and the distribution of men and women in various employment categories on campus

2. Recommend policies, procedures, organizational arrangements, and special services that would enhance the opportunities of women to achieve their personal and professional goals at CMU

3. Suggest the outlines of an affirmative action program designed to correct or ameliorate any discriminatory practices or unequal conditions discovered in the commission's study

4. Recommend a continuing vehicle for monitoring the implementation of an affirmative action plan and to suggest which offices within the university should be responsible for various aspects of implementation.

The commission functioned as an objective investigatory body, leaving the advocacy function to women's groups on the campus.

Throughout the eight months of its existence, meetings were held at
least weekly, including both public and confidential hearings with
campus administrators, representatives of women's groups, and concerned individuals. The commission's research director collected
voluminous statistical data on working conditions, distributions,
and salaries of women employed at CMU. She was aided in her task
by the fact that two key administrators were members of the commission.

A preliminary report was submitted to the president near the
end of April 1971, and, at his request, to all deans, department
heads, and directors with a request for written comments. Many
members of the campus community did respond; and the commission
spent the summer evaluating these comments, doing more analysis
of the data already obtained, collecting additional data, and doing
some follow-up inquiries prior to submitting its final report to the
president. The Final Report, published in November 1971, contained
155 pages of information about the status and needs of women faculty,
students, and staff, plus 55 recommendations for corrective actions
organized around the following observations:

1. Records are incomplete and inconsistent, communication of
information is poor
2. Women are underrepresented in faculty and administrative
positions
3. Women are underrepresented on decision-making bodies
4. Women are paid less than men for the same work
5. There is a decline in educational opportunities for women at
CMU.[1]

The commission's Final Report also devoted a chapter to a description of the kind of administrative office it thought could best implement its recommendations. This was essentially the same recommendation with which the original women's group had begun a request
that the university set up an implementing office to "equalize the
status of women," to ensure "equal opportunity," and to promote "affirmative action."

1971-72

During the year following publication of the commission's Final
Report, several events combined to slow the momentum generated
while it was in preparation. First, several key leaders left the campus, including the university president and the vice-president to whom
he had given responsibility for establishing an Affirmative Action Of-

fice. The commission itself disbanded; and members returned to their duties as teachers, administrators, or staff. Although the acting president (who had been a member of the commission) appointed a committee to draft an affirmative action plan and a monitoring commission to report on progress toward implementing the commission recommendations, the campus atmosphere was one of uncertainty and rumor, a poor climate for new programs. The university was also in the grip of a serious financial problem that caused administrators to direct their efforts toward issues other than affirmative action.

This interim period ended in July 1972, when the new president took office. His overriding problem, of course, was the financial crisis; among the nonfinancial issues that he inherited was the commission's recommendation for an Affirmative Action Office, a recommendation now pressed doggedly by a few women. During the fall of 1972, the president appointed a search committee for an affirmative action officer, and by the end of the semester the office became a reality. The Affirmative Action Office began functioning on January 15, 1973.

THE AFFIRMATIVE ACTION OFFICE: JANUARY 1973-MARCH 1974

This part of the CMU story concerns procedures and problems related to implementation of affirmative action. While the effort from September 1970 through December 1972 was largely "diagnostic," the activities since January 1973 have been primarily "treatment"—an effort that is a long way from being complete.

Resources

In the year and a half between publication of the commission's Final Report and the establishment of the Affirmative Action Office, the women's groups that had been responsible for the beginning of "the movement" at CMU had largely disbanded. Individual faculty women were turning away from social action to concentrate on their own research, others had left the community, and a few had obtained challenging new positions that demanded most of their energies. Initial efforts to revive the old organization or create a new one were unsuccessful. The old leaders felt they had done all, and more, than could be expected of them; and now that the university finally had a paid affirmative action officer, she should take on the struggle. Indeed, several women seemed to view the affirmative action officer as their "friend in court," and were inclined to feel betrayed if she

could not deliver special programs and professional rewards that
they wanted.

If lack of organized support from campus women was the first
surprise, the rather meager support that the university could provide
in the midst of its heroic belt-tightening was another. The Affirmative Action Office was lovely, located on the executive floor of the
administration building; however, except for occasional help from
graduate students, the staff was shared with another administrator
and the time demands on the affirmative action officer were stringent.
She did report directly to the president, which gave clout to the position in the perception of some colleagues; but the office's budget was
included in that for the president's office, which effectively buried
from general scrutiny the small amount set aside for affirmative action. One might say it was a low-budget, high-profile office, the
sort of operation that stimulates critics to cry tokenism—but one that
also can be understood as an effort to do as much as possible with as
little expense as possible, relying on display and politics where money
and staff are limited.

Strategies

Given a limited paid staff, it seemed obvious that efforts should
be made to involve volunteers and line administrators as much as
possible to extend the effectiveness of the office. Accordingly, two
advisory councils were appointed, one for women and one for minorities, drawing membership from various campus constituencies.
Task forces from the councils met and studied specific areas, such
as problems of women graduate students, goals for minority faculty,
and fringe benefits. In addition, since it seemed desirable to get
line administrators to do the major implementation of affirmative action programs, with the affirmative action officer concentrating on
monitoring and resources, a revision of the affirmative action plan
was begun to incorporate specific administrators. Finally, the affirmative action officer became a member of several university committees, such as the Faculty Senate Council on Faculty Affairs and
the Carnegie-Mellon Action Program Steering Committee. These
three concepts still constitute working strategies for the office.

Accomplishments

Much remains to be done in affirmative action at CMU, and any
discussion of accomplishments seems decidedly premature. Still,
some progress has been made and more is planned, enough to war-

rant at least brief mention here—in part because without it, the later
material on problems in this paper would be misleadingly pessimistic,
and in part because it may be useful to other affirmative action officers. The accomplishments of the Affirmative Action Office have
been organized around the five categories into which the commission
grouped its 55 recommendations.

Records Are Incomplete and Inconsistent, Communication of Information Is Poor

The Affirmative Action Office has been included as a user of the
normal flow of management information, such as registrar's data,
Admissions Office statistics, equal employment opportunity reports,
and announcements of new job openings. When deficiencies in data-
collecting appeared, they were corrected immediately where this was
possible (for example, recording sex of applicants to graduate programs). In other instances the compilation of needed records required
fairly extensive changes in procedures of information-gathering or
-recording. For example, it is obvious that in order to determine
whether men and women staff workers are paid equally for equal work,
one needs a system of determining equality of jobs—a good job classification system. At CMU the new administration is updating the job
classification system, a process to which the Affirmative Action Office
has input at several points, including a review of the system for possible bias. Until this task is completed, salary analyses must be considered tentative.

Women Are Underrepresented in Faculty and Administrative Positions

The most systematic method for increasing the number of women
in faculty and administrative positions is to develop numerical goals
based on their availability in the appropriate labor markets, as recommended in Revised Order 4 and by the HEW Higher Education Guidelines[2] (1972). Because college faculty members are both intelligent
and argumentative, however, it is essential that goals be set that
have strong logical bases, and that plenty of time be allowed for discussion and debate with deans and department heads. At CMU it
took six months of such activity to set our goals for women faculty.
The value of this lengthy process is evident from the fact that the
goals, timetables, and recruitment procedures finally produced have
been accepted almost matter-of-factly by the department heads. (Perhaps by the time the goals became policy, everyone was bored by debate and resigned to their inevitability.)

Separate goals are needed for women staff in administrative positions because of differences in the availability of women in academic and nonacademic labor pools. Until the goals are set, hiring of women staff must proceed on a job-by-job basis, and has included the appointment or promotion of women to such positions as associate dean of engineering, manager of the university libraries, and assistant director of estate planning.

Women Are Underrepresented on Decision-Making Bodies

The principal reason why women are underrepresented on decision-making university bodies is that membership on such bodies is frequently ex officio, and women do not hold their share of administrative offices. Thus, the long-range solution is to get more women into the administrative pipeline. In the meantime, it is possible to look for women to fill decision-making positions that are not ex officio—such as officers in the Faculty Senate or staff organization. In addition, of course, the affirmative action officer can and should serve on many committees ex officio; the problem here is that the multitude of decision-making committees far exceeds the energies of any one person. The sending of delegates from the Affirmative Action Office to such committees represents one interim solution.

Women Are Paid Less Than Men for the Same Work

The first step toward monitoring salaries of women faculty is to obtain good data on current and proposed salaries and on historical percentage increments. Since most of this information is prepared routinely for annual budget review, the simplest way to see it is for the affirmative action officer to become a member of the Budget Review Committee. Once on the committee, however, with full access to salary data, the real problem begins: the problem of rationalizing faculty salaries. Here I only want to caution new affirmative action officers to be sure they enter budget review sessions with detailed information on experience, publications, teaching evaluations, and the like for at least a few key women faculty whose salaries are low. Without such data one is forced to argue from the weak and easily demolished position that no woman faculty member's salary should be below the male average.

There Is a Decline in Educational Opportunities for Women

In its Final Report the commission noted the steady decline in educational programs for women at CMU, citing the successive elimination of the schools of social work and library science, and the wo-

men's college. It suggested that when women faculty and students are
in the majority in an educational program, the program tends to be
perceived as academically weak; and this perceived weakness becomes
the justification for first limiting its resources and eventually phasing
it out. The two assumptions in this reasoning are that the perception
of weakness is a reflection of sexist bias, and that decisions about
curricula are made in terms of the strength or weakness of programs.
Although it is great fun to argue about the first assumption, it would
be better to put the issue to empirical test. It would be an interesting piece of research, for example, to ask deans to evaluate two identical curricula, one for men and one for women, as a step toward
determining whether sexism influences such judgments.

The second assumption, that decisions to continue or to terminate
programs are based on perceptions of their academic strength or
weakness, probably is less true today, when declining enrollments
force universities to tailor their curricula more carefully to the demands of educational consumers than it was during the affluent 1960s—
when masses of students competed to be accepted into whatever programs the university chose to offer. Within the limitations imposed
by the nature of their resources, it seems likely that universities today will strive to develop programs that bring in students and research support, regardless of whether the students are male or female. If I am correct here, it means that today, more than ever,
university administrations will respond to increased demands from
potential women students by finding curricula to meet their educational needs. For affirmative action officers the logical strategy is
to work at identifying such needs and creating such demand among
high school women. As one example, CMU has actively advertised
for women engineering students through television spots, written material, and career conferences. One measure of our success is the
increase from 3.12 to 7.2 percent women among our undergraduate
engineering students over the past four years.

Special Projects

Although space does not permit detailed description, it should be
mentioned that many hours of Affirmative Action Office time have gone
into developing special supportive programs where the need was obvious. Other universities will find other lacunae in their support services; at CMU we needed and have developed gynecological services,
a lecture series on human sexuality, a maternity-leave policy in compliance with Equal Education Opportunity Commission guidelines, a
women students' collective, improved pension arrangements for
staff employees, and increased publicity for women's activities. Al-

though I view these projects as necessary, they are peripheral to the main Affirmative Action Office thrust of concerns for fair recruitment, salaries, and working conditions. However, it should be noted that special projects usually make better news copy than do employment issues, and all affirmative action officers need good campus publicity.

PROBLEMS AND ATTEMPTS AT SOLUTIONS

I would like to discuss next some of the problems that I have encountered as affirmative action officer at CMU. Where possible, I will also mention whatever solutions I have found effective. The problems fall naturally into two general categories: institutional problems that arise from the nature of universities and the nature of affirmative action, and interpersonal problems reflecting attitudinal conflicts about changes in the established system.

Institutional Problems

A number of economic factors combine to make this a particularly poor time for affirmative action. As everyone knows, low enrollments and limited research funds are forcing universities to retrench. Budget cuts, efforts to restrict tenure, faculty salaries held below cost-of-living levels—all these are familiar themes. The present austerity comes on the heels of a decade of enthusiastic production of graduate students, many of whom are now unable to find jobs in the constricted academic marketplace. Aside from the obvious fact that there are fewer jobs for women as well as for men, this general state of affairs means that affirmative action activities that bring in no money and may, in fact, add to university costs, can come to be viewed by budget-conscious administrators as inimicable to the first priority of the university: solvency. More troublesome is the fact that with dozens of applicants for every faculty position, deans and department heads can now afford to sit back and wait for superstars to emerge from their collection of candidates. If the superstar is a woman, they probably will have no objection; but it is very hard for them to give up this "buyer's market" of overqualified candidates in order to abide by affirmative action goals.

I have not yet discovered a full solution to this problem, and doubt that one exists. One partial solution is to educate administrators to the loss of research funds they risk if they fail to comply with government legislation. I might note that although the poor economic climate makes affirmative action more difficult, it also makes it more essential because recruitment operations within the current market, unconstrained by affirmative action, might well produce even higher percentages of male faculty than we now find in universities.

Another problem results from the fact that universities, especially selective private universities, have not traditionally used quantitative, objective measures of determining faculty qualifications or of assessing performance. This is a particularly bothersome problem for salary analyses. After struggling with the matter at several salary review meetings, I am somewhat reluctantly coming to the conclusion that we need to develop statistical models of the determinants of faculty salaries—models from which it will be possible to determine statistically the effect of sex on salary, all other factors being held equal. This type of analysis has been reported in the literature.[3] At CMU we are currently developing a statistical model to determine the influence of sex on salaries of individual faculty members. (See Chapter 6.)

Attitudinal Problems

It probably is inevitable that the work of the affirmative action officer, directed as it is toward bringing about changes in traditional patterns of occupational status, will encounter resentment and hostility from those who are threatened by departures from the old order. Perhaps less obviously inevitable is the subtle interference that arises from the actions of those who stand to benefit from affirmative action efforts and are, indeed, overtly friendly to women's rights.

Troublesome attitudes come from both men and women. From men, the most obvious resistance comes from administrators who resent my "interference" with their operation. The form varies from outright hostility to more subtle foot-dragging or attempts to co-opt the Affirmative Action Office. The DeFunis case, now declared moot by the Supreme Court, was godsend to opponents of affirmative action. For example, I had a small "memo war" with one administrator who mailed copies of briefs favoring DeFunis to me, the deans, the president, and other administrators across campus. Probably the best response to this sort of thing is to remain cool, proceed with one's job, and send off countermemos if time permits.

Another form of resistance is reflected in the refusal to accept evidence of sex discrimination without exhaustive analysis of all possible alternatives. A typical argument here is that even though men and women with identical job classifications are paid unequally, the difference in salaries may indicate bad job classifications, differences in seniority, or differences in the "real" value of the work performed, rather than sex discrimination. Although it is tempting to treat such arguments as so much static in the system and to ignore them as one sets up salary equalization plans, such a strategy is not always possible if the administrators involved are influential. It also may change the system less than the development of academically impeccable statistical methods to identify salary determinants. Though it is tiresome, it may be necessary to prove the obvious.

Finally, the negative attitudes of male colleagues can have a damaging effect on the morale and energies of the affirmative action officer, especially if her position isolates her from daily contact with the men and women who support her objectives. If my only working relationships were with individuals whose operations I have been appointed to police, I probably would soon become susceptible to the co-opting effect of being praised by them for not doing my job. To guard against this possibility, it is essential that the affirmative action officer stay in frequent contact with feminist groups and individuals. I have found it personally helpful to have an informal "cabinet" of women whose judgments I trust and to whom I turn periodically for catharsis, refueling, and encouragement.

Problems also arise in dealing with other women. I have already mentioned the women who view me as their "friend in court" and look to me for special favors. To some extent this is a realistic view; I am working to promote the legitimate interests of women. But it is unrealistic to expect that one person can take personal action regarding the grievance of each individual woman. To avoid being expected to perform the impossible and bitterly criticized for having "sold out" when one inevitably fails to deliver, it probably is an excellent idea for the affirmative action officer to develop or improve university grievance procedures and direct women petitioners to use them.

NOTES

1. U.S. Department of Health, Education and Welfare, Higher Education Guidelines (Washington, D.C.: Department of Health, Education and Welfare, Office of the Secretary, Office for Civil Rights, 1972).

2. Commission on the Status and Needs of Women at CMU, Final Report (Pittsburgh: CMU, 1971).

3. Nancy M. Gordon, Thomas E. Morton, and Ina C. Braden, "Faculty Salaries: Is There Discrimination by Sex, Race, and Discipline?" American Economic Review 64 (June 1974): 419; Raymond N. Kieft, "Are Your Salaries 'Equal'?" College Management, April 1974.

10

**AFFIRMATIVE ACTION
AT STANFORD
UNIVERSITY**
Introductory Notes
by Anne S. Miner

INTRODUCTORY NOTES

Affirmative action programs and plans—not to mention the underlying notions about their value and purposes—are not static. By the
time this book has been published, the written affirmative action plan
for Stanford will have undergone another cycle of review, planned ad-
ditions will have been adopted, and operational improvements in the
implementation of the program will have been made. Also, anticipated changes in the plan may be needed to reflect emerging national
issues and/or specific situations arising at Stanford.

Even more important, an affirmative action plan is just that—a
plan (a written statement of intent and procedure to move toward objectives). The quality of the plan is a necessary, but not sufficient,
context for judging the quality of an affirmative action program (the
integrity and quality of actual day-to-day decisions affecting professional or employment opportunity).

For these reasons I have included some personal comments regarding the components and style of the written affirmative action
plan for Stanford, some examples of issues now being studied in more
detail at Stanford (about which the reader can anticipate comment in
future plans), and some notes on the uses and limits of written affirmative action plans in general.*

---

*The reader should clearly understand that these introductory
notes reflect my personal judgments and beliefs; they are not necessarily the institutional views or policies of Stanford University.

The 1973-74 Written Plan at Stanford

Not everyone is fascinated by the ins and outs of formal written affirmative action planning (work-force analyses, specification of responsibility, audit systems, goals, documentation of selection criteria, and so on). However, it is important to view the material reproduced here as part of a larger written document and in the context of its purposes.

The text of the 1973-74 Stanford plan pertaining to faculty has been printed here. The main text was published as a supplement to the Stanford Campus Report, which is distributed to about 12,000 people. All four volumes of the plan were placed in Stanford's library and, of course, were forwarded to the Department of Health, Education and Welfare as Stanford's written response to its contractual obligations under Executive Order 11375.

Some broad priorities shaped the plan's style. They were similar to the ideas that shaped its precursor, the 1972-73 plan. (In 1972-73, Stanford published its first omnibus affirmative action plan, describing all employment-related programs. In prior years, various separate planning documents regarding faculty or staff employment or construction work on campus had been published, approved by the trustees or president, and/or forwarded to HEW.) Some of the rough guidelines used in preparing the 1973-74 plan and its precursor were the following:

- The plan should provide a comprehensive policy framework about affirmative action in employment matters—a framework that will stand over time.
- It would make sense to the interested, but nonexpert, reader.
- Its primary purposes should be formally communicating to officers, managers, faculty, and employees the basic policies and procedures of affirmative action, suggesting areas of success, and identifying broad problem areas of importance to Stanford.
- It should stand as the formal plan submitted to the federal government, meeting technical requirements for an affirmative action plan.
- It should be morally and legally sound.

While these guidelines seem obvious, the open publication of the formal written plan did represent a somewhat unusual approach in 1972-73. The guidelines remain difficult to satisfy in any one document; a plan covering every item noted in Executive Order 11375, for example, simply cannot be a short, easy-to-read document.

Some lawyers and administrators (including myself) find comprehensive affirmative action plans not only valuable and necessary, but actually interesting. Many employees and faculty members, however, seek more specific information about their own immediate role in the program and how it will likely affect their fates. Future reports at Stanford will no doubt reflect that need.

Evolving Issues and Practices

A complete description of additional procedures or policies evolving at Stanford would end up as a revised affirmative action plan —there are many. Two examples of new developments that will most likely be reported in the next Stanford report might be of interest, however.

Several important issues in faculty appointment procedures here (and elsewhere) had previously been referred to a special Committee on the Professoriate at Stanford. The committee's mission was not to study affirmative action issues specifically; but it did address issues central to affirmative action. Some of its recommendations and resulting procedures now approved or under review by the Faculty Senate include the following:

- All junior faculty members should have an annual opportunity to discuss with the department chairman the department's evaluation of the quality of their work (before the year of the final tenure decision), at the option of the faculty member.
- Formal documentation of decisions not to grant tenure should be prepared monthly, and this documentation forwarded to university officers who normally review positive recommendations.
- Schools and departments should formulate and communicate more explicitly the normal criteria for positive tenure decisions in their disciplines.

In the staff employment area a special study was done in 1973 of problems and patterns affecting administrative/professional jobs paying more than about $12,000 per year. A task force was established to review upward mobility and career development for all professional/administrative employees at Stanford (and affirmative action in that context), and most likely will develop several options for change that may involve no policy changes but will lead to additional concrete support for managers in matching internal employees with promotional opportunities, and in finding talented external applicants for such jobs (including minority and/or female applicants).

Finally, of course, as with all plans for any administrative goal, the technical aspects of the plan continue to evolve. In future plans, for example, the staff goal-setting procedure will be revised—cer-

tainly to increase accuracy and timeliness, and to reduce the enormous amount of rote numerical tasks performed by departments, and,
one hopes, to engage in goal-setting only when it is meaningful and
useful. Similarly, the faculty goal-setting method most likely will
be revised for future plans.

Notes on Written Plans Versus Actual Programs

It is axiomatic that policies, by themselves, do not necessarily
produce ready action—unless, I suppose, they are outright commands
unilaterally enforced at all levels. It is also axiomatic that not all
action is useful or good.

Even after reviewing a fairly detailed affirmative action plan,
it is important to say: "Well, that's the plan; what about the quality
of the program? Does the plan have any effect? More important, is
the effect important and valuable?"

What factors should be considered in evaluating the quality of the
program, beyond the plan? Obviously, one issue is the level and
quality of involvement of senior officers. Involvement here means
more than general goodwill and official accountability; it means so-
phistication and breadth, creativity and interest. In the question of
so-called "negative tenure" decisions, for example, active initiative
and thoughtful analyses by senior academic officers at Stanford were
required, so that both equity and academic integrity would be served
in the formation of new procedures.

Other important issues to consider in reviewing a program include the following:

Is the institution credible in the acknowledgment of the most fundamental aspects of employment equity? Has it accomplished in a
timely way such ideologically "remedial" (but administratively time-
consuming) tasks as achieving salary equity by sex and developing
job-related selection criteria for staff jobs? Is the plan having any
effect other than adding paper work?

Beyond basic procedures does the institution have an informed
and coherent sense of what all the affirmative action procedures,
goals, and debates are for? Does the sense of its purpose go beyond
either legal defense (not a bad motivator, but thoroughly inadequate
as the sole driving force) or paternalism (which is a potentially dan-
gerous driving force)? If so, are there intelligent priorities among
affirmative action objectives (procedural or otherwise)?

Is there evidence that officers, managers, and senior faculty
have begun to address the evolving issues that arise in a pluralistic
institution? In nonacademic employment, to give a similar example,
casual lunches, poker games, or a drink after work traditionally

may have provided informal training and critical feedback for young, white, male professionals. If these same mechanisms are not automatically available for women or minority employees in a particular group, have other channels that provide the same opportunity for learning been developed? Among faculty, is there evidence that new faculty (particularly, but not only, minority and/or female members) know and understand the more subtle criteria on which they will be evaluated for tenure? If not, what kind of changes (formal or informal) would be appropriate to assure that they do?

Even a good written plan does not, and cannot, answer all of these questions. The key to a good program, perhaps, is the balance between continuously framing or acknowledging problems and acting in the context of current reality. On the whole, I believe that the balance achieved at Stanford between attending to form and to substance has been good. Institutional evolution of any sort moves slowly, however; and I believe the plan here is an appropriate, but not the final, response of Stanford University to the broadest issue of equity, quality, and diversity within this particular institution of higher education.

STANFORD UNIVERSITY AFFIRMATIVE ACTION REPORT

The purpose of affirmative action programs is to provide effective equal opportunity in all aspects of employment: hiring, compensation, promotion, and tenure. This document reports on the implementation of Stanford's affirmative action plan during 1972-73 and describes its present designs for future development.

Introduction

A recent volume of essays,* sponsored by the Carnegie Commission on Higher Education, summed up its description of Stanford University this way:

> By any of the ordinary indices—growth in facilities
> or budget, faculty distinction, the test socres of success-
> ful applicants, or the American Council on Education
> ratings of graduate programs—Stanford rose [in the

*David Riesman and Verne A. Stadtman, Academic Transformation (New York: McGraw-Hill, 1973). See John Walsh, "Stanford's Search for Solutions," Ch. 14, p. 321.

years since World War II] to a place among the best half-
dozen American universities and is still, on top of it, a
marvelously pleasant place.

Stanford's academic organization, its commitments to excellence
in teaching and research, its diminished capacity for growth, and its
rural/suburban setting combine to shape the institution and its policies.

The university is organized into seven schools, each with a high
degree of autonomy in academic matters: Earth Sciences, Education,
Engineering, Graduate School of Business, Humanities and Sciences,
Law, and Medicine. In addition the Stanford Linear Accelerator Center (SLAC), operated as a national facility by Stanford for the Atomic
Energy Commission, a number of other laboratories, programs, and
institutes, and various administrative offices fall outside of school
jurisdiction. Employment policies and practices in all these areas
are a part of the university's overall affirmative action plan, with
basic employment decisions delegated to schools and departments; a
system of checks and balances assures that those decisions are consistent with the university's overall objectives.

The Stanford University Hospital on the main campus is a separate legal entity, but it has joined with the university in a unified plan
for affirmative action. In the main it has implemented the university's
affirmative action plan with only minor variations. Although the legal
and contractual obligations of the hospital are not identical with those
of the campus, a summary of its actions is included in this report as
part of the university's voluntary program.

Stanford was established in 1885 by Senator Leland Stanford and
his wife as a memorial to their son, Leland Stanford, Jr., on 8,000
acres of prime ranch land in Santa Clara County. That location influences Stanford's educational opportunities and its employment picture
as well. Although faculty and some senior staff positions are filled
from the national and international marketplace, most of the staff is
drawn from a suburban labor force.

In autumn 1972, there were 6,412 undergraduate students and
4,962 graduate students at Stanford. There were 1,080 professional-
ranked members of the Academic Council, 255 instructors and other
salaried teaching personnel, and a nonacademic staff of about 6,000,
including those at SLAC. In addition, about 2,500 employees work at
the hospital.

The 1972 figures vary only slightly from those of 1971 used in
the university's affirmative action plan of July 1972. This fact de-
monstrates an important present-day characteristic of Stanford. After 20 years of constant, often rapid, growth, Stanford has reached
a stabilized size; and while there may be changes in the direction and
balance of education, major shifts in emphasis are unlikely.

This report and plan concern employment, but it is useful to relate affirmative action to students, a university constituency that distinguishes Stanford from other kinds of organizations.

From the time Stanford opened until World War II, the students came largely from prosperous Western families. The rush of World War II veterans in 1945 marked the first significant change in the university's student body, and represented a mix of ages and backgrounds that reverted in the 1950s to the more familiar student profile. Stanford changed significantly in the 1960s.

Minority Students

In 1966 the university initiated a recruiting program for black students with high potential, a beginning that was strengthened after April 1968, following the assassination of Martin Luther King. Locally as well as nationally, there was a surge of public discussion of racism, civil rights, and the role of major institutions in the nation's racial patterns of opportunity. The following year, Stanford's effort broadened to include increased Chicano student representation and, in 1970, native Americans. Traditionally there has been an outstanding group of Asian-American students at Stanford. Over the past four years this number has almost doubled.

Within the framework of Stanford's institutional commitment to improve its minority representation, the undergraduate admissions office and those of each professional school have worked out minority recruiting and admissions procedures that are consistent with their academic objectives and standards.

In 1973, at the direction of President Lyman, a university-wide review of minority student programs was undertaken in order to use the experiences of the various schools as the basis for improved performance in the future. Reminding the community that the general commitment to improve the representation of ethnic and racial minorities had been implemented in different ways, President Lyman said: "There is much diversity in the way various offices around the campus approach minority programs. This is wholly appropriate. We are not seeking uniformity so long as we understand the principles which underlie our efforts, and we keep in communication."

In May, Robert Rosenzweig, vice-provost and adviser to the president, summarized the various reports submitted as part of that survey in a report to the entire community, expressing the hope that the paper would serve as a basis for continuing discussion of a complex subject. At the undergraduate level there were 637 minority students enrolled in the fall of 1972. They represented 9.9 percent of the total undergraduates and included 294 blacks, 296 Chicanos, and 47 native Americans. There were also 314 Asian-Americans.

Since 1968-69, the total number of black and Chicano graduate students at Stanford has increased from 77 to 400, while total graduate enrollment has declined slightly (5,244 to 4,962). There are also about 100 Asian-American and 22 native American graduate students.

A committee, originally headed by Maria Baeza and Thomas Rhue of the office of the dean of graduate studies, is compiling a study of Stanford graduate education for minority students, which should be a useful guide to future policy-making. Based on data collected from questionnaires sent to all graduate minority students, the report should be available during 1973. The material covers a range of subjects—admissions, financial aid, undergraduate background—and is expected to be useful to a number of other institutions as well as Stanford.

The affairs of ethnic minority students at Stanford generally have been incorporated into appropriate functional offices rather than into a structure designed around a particular constituency. Therefore, the admissions and financial aid offices, the counseling service, the deans of graduate and undergraduate study, the dean of student affairs, and the deans of the professional schools deal with these questions for all students; in some cases, minority-group members within the office are available to work with minority groups as part of their general responsibilities.

Women Students

In response to a lengthy study by the Academic Council Committee on Undergraduate Admissions and Financial Aid and a Faculty Senate decision adopted without dissent in June 1972, the board of trustees in September 1972 initiated legal proceedings to modify the founding grant. When Stanford opened, the founding grant stated that it was open to men and women alike. In 1899, Mrs. Stanford, bothered by the possibility that the number of women might exceed that of men in an institution dedicated to the memory of her son, amended the grant to limit women to 500. In 1933, responding to the increased total enrollment, the board of trustees established a 60-40 ratio, which was faithful to the balance Mrs. Stanford had sought in establishing a 500-women limit. In March 1973, the Santa Clara County Superior Court removed the amendments to the grant; and the trustee resolution of 1933 was rescinded, making it technically final that no quota exists for admission of women and that sex is not a factor in the admission process.

Although sex had not been a criterion in admission in recent years, the changes were sought, in part, because it was widely believed that there was a limit on the number of women Stanford would admit to a freshman class. The Committee on Undergraduate Admissions and Financial Aid has attempted to minimize or eliminate artificial restrictions in the admissions process. Within the framework of limited enrollment, high standards, and desired diversity, all candidates should have an equal opportunity of competing for admission to the university. From 1965 to 1971, the university's undergraduate enrollment increased 10 percent; during that period, men's enrollment dropped by 1 percent, while women's enrollment increased 36 percent. The entering class for 1973 includes 913 men and 582 women.

Graduate Women

The number of women and minority students in graduate programs was the subject of months of deliberation in the Faculty Senate during 1973. The Study of Graduate Education at Stanford, published in 1972, included a paper on the subject of women graduate students; the Baeza/Rhue committee, mentioned earlier, is separately considering minority graduate students. The Committee on the Education and Employment of Women also submitted a report on graduate admissions. After extensive discussion of these two reports, the Senate in May adopted a resolution calling upon all graduate programs to publicize opportunities for women and minority students in graduate study and to seek applicants from those groups. It also directed the dean of graduate studies to provide coordinating assistance in these efforts and to report annually to the Senate on progress.

This resolution by the Senate was the first institution-wide commitment to increase numbers of women in graduate programs, although individual schools (Engineering, Business, and Medicine) had begun active recruiting of women candidates. A widely publicized pamphlet was published by the School of Engineering in the summer of 1972, which encouraged women to seek careers in engineering; this followed a 1971 publication by the School of Medicine. In 1973, the physics department directed a leaflet, "Women in Physics," to women undergraduates.

The Committee on the Education and Employment of Women has been a continuing source of information and advice to the university on women's affairs. CEEW, established in 1970, is one of eight standing university committees that are appointed by, and primarily responsible to, the president. They deal with matters on which the responsibility for recommendation or action is diffused among different constituencies. CEEW has worked on a broad charge but has been involved primarily in student affairs, including preprofessional counseling. A report, "The Stanford Woman in 1972," based on a survey of senior women in the spring of 1972, was published in the winter of 1972-73.

There are, in addition, various other informal advocate mechanisms—both groups, such as caucuses of women and minority students
in schools and departments, and individual employees and faculty members—that have raised important issues or focused attention on problems of the education and employment of minorities and women.

In January 1973, a study on child care prepared by Aimee Leifer,
former acting assistant professor at Stanford, was published. Provost William Miller and Vice-President for Business and Finance
Robert Augsburger, in a policy statement regarding the report, said
that Stanford can and should facilitate workable child-care arrangements for faculty, staff, and students, but that the university would
not now commit further funds to directly design, construct, or manage day-care centers. The dean of student affairs was designated to
coordinate the university's facilitation of child care; his office will
collect, maintain, and disseminate information on services available
in the area. The university currently provides space for the child-
care center of the Stanford community.

*   *   *   *   *

The discussion of students above suggests a vital aspect of Stanford's affirmative action employment program: the need for broad
representation of women and members of ethnic minority groups
within the faculty and staff to improve the quality of a Stanford education. The university's responsibility to its students to provide effective and appropriate counseling and role models has been a determining factor of priorities for affirmative action. The character of the
program, as represented in this document, has been strongly influenced by those educational priorities.

The obligation to students, however, is only one of the forces
that shape the priorities of Stanford's plan. Another effort is less
tangible. Stanford has attempted, particularly since 1968, in ways
that are appropriate to its educational role, to help this nation overcome and solve some of the devastating effects of racism in the society as a whole. The university has tried to be a responsible neigh-
bor to its nearby minority communities through work with Urban Co-
alition to provide some campus housing for low- and medium-income
groups and the Youth Opportunity Program, a work/counseling experience for high school students. Through research and teaching,
faculty and students have pursued solutions to societal problems of
poverty and urbanization. But Stanford's primary educational mission
is to educate and train students for leadership roles, some of whom
will return to their own ethnic communities. While Stanford University, compared with public institutions, will never be a source of
mass education, the impact of the minority students it does educate
should be significant.

By involving minority administrators in university management, by bringing in young minority faculty members, and by launching new minority professionals, Stanford broadens the national pool of capable leaders for careers in this and other institutions.

The other critical determinant of Stanford's affirmative action plan for employment is the complex, evolving body of laws and procedures aimed at nondiscrimination. Two elements are particularly critical: Title VII of the Civil Rights Act, administered by the EEOC, and Executive Order 11375, which applies to all federal contractors. The Department of Health, Education and Welfare monitors compliance with the executive order by universities. The Atomic Energy Commission has the primary monitoring responsibility for its contractors, SLAC among them. The Stanford University Hospital program, in this context, is voluntary, since it is not subject to the executive order and its employees are not university employees.

In response to federal requirements, Stanford University submitted various affirmative action planning documents to HEW and AEC during the past five years. In July 1972 a revised, comprehensive affirmative action report and plan, which the university has been asked to implement, were sent to HEW (and distributed to the Stanford community). Some of the revisions included in this report and plan reflect HEW's assistance and suggestions. While the total plan is responsive to federal orders, it also contains components that go beyond the legal requirements.

Reaffirmation of Policy

The foundation of all policy at Stanford University is the institution's determination to maintain itself as a university of the highest quality. Implicit in that tenet—as explicitly and regularly affirmed—is the university's policy of providing equal opportunity for all employees and applicants for employment regardless of race, color, creed, religion, national origin, age, or sex, except where sex or age is a bona fide occupational qualification.

The plan for affirmative action described here is intended, in ways that are consistent with both those premises, to increase the number and to improve the relative position of minority-group members and women on the Stanford faculty and staff. And while proportional representation by race and sex is not necessary in every institution in a pluralistic society, Stanford's educational goals are best served if the institution reflects pluralism at all levels.

The university has frequently stated its policy of equal employment opportunity. To the extent that the term signals a commitment to avoid discrimination in personnel decisions, it intends to remain

an equal opportunity employer. It is demonstrable, however, that
the avoidance of direct discrimination, even where that can be fully
achieved, does not by itself necessarily produce changes in the composition of the faculty or staff.

To achieve such changes does, indeed, require affirmative action. Hiring decisions that seem to be neutral are not nondiscriminatory if the applicant pool does not include women and minority-group
members. The traditional "old boy" networks for establishing criteria, locating applicants, and making recommendations can perpetuate
the existing hierarchy. Positive recruiting is, therefore, basic. The
need for careful review of stated qualifications goes hand in hand with
open recruiting. Necessary attention to applicants' qualifications has
too often resulted in rigid reliance on degree and experience requirements that artificially and improperly exclude from consideration
members of minority groups and women who could assume the responsibilities of a vacant position.

Stanford is determined to maintain an institutional awareness of
the many aspects of the problem until it is clear that normal mechanisms automatically safeguard the appropriate direction.

The university is committed to an affirmative action program that
consists, in part, of the following elements: (1) a requirement for
imaginative and serious search and recruiting; (2) administrative review of hiring practices; (3) analysis of faculty and staff units to determine problem areas; (4) identification of, and response to, undesirable practices; (5) facilitation of training, where possible and consistent with the educational objectives, that permits personal development sufficient for entry to some positions and promotion to others.

Stanford's officers who are responsible for affirmative action
believe that these procedures will make Stanford University an affirmative action employer in the best sense of that phrase and will improve the representation of women and minority-group members in
the faculty and staff.

Responsibility for Development and Implementation

The president of the University, Richard W. Lyman, bears the
ultimate responsibility for the implementation of Stanford's affirmative action plan. He has delegated that responsibility, including development of numerical goals, when appropriate, to each of the senior officers of the university within their respective areas of authority. Thus, regular line responsibilities include affirmative action
and, beyond the vice-president, the program follows the direct line
of authority through the deans and department heads. There are
three basically separate organizations in terms of implementation:
faculty, staff, and external affirmative action.

Professor Arthur Bienenstock, vice-provost for faculty affairs, is charged with the responsibility for the development and coordination of faculty affirmative action.

Emil Sarpa, director of personnel and employee relations, is responsible for the aspects of staff affirmative action that depend upon the functions of the university personnel office. Recruiting, training opportunities, criteria validation, job classification, job parity, and compensation schedules are coordinated and centered in his office. Douglas Dupen, director of personnel at SLAC, and James Moore, director of personnel at the hospital, are responsible for these functions at those two locations.

Vice-President for Business and Finance Robert Augsburger is responsible for external affirmative action by which Stanford, as a purchaser of goods and services, positively affects the employment and hiring practices of its contractors, principally those in construction.

Anne S. Miner, university affirmative action officer, provides coordination between the faculty and staff programs, and support for the principal officers and their line managers in terms of staff affirmative action. In addition, she is Stanford's official liaison officer with outside compliance agencies and one of several university officers who work with minority and women's groups. An additional staff member, Anthony Alarid, was appointed in January 1973. The affirmative action office was, from the outset, temporary in nature. It was established to help the university revise its affirmative action program. By 1974-75 the plan should be sufficiently integrated into management that a separate officer for the overall program may no longer be necessary.

Coordinators for staff affirmative action were appointed during 1972-73 for broad areas within the university and, on behalf of the appropriate vice-president, dean, or officer, were given responsibility for coordinating the development and implementation of the staff program within these areas.

In several cases advisory groups have been formed to advise and assist these officers. Two new panels—one for internal affirmative action and one for the external affirmative action program—have been appointed by the president.

The membership includes faculty administrative officers charged with specific affirmative action responsibilities and other individuals who can provide special expertise and resources. The vice-president for medical affairs has an advisory committee made up of Medical School and hospital employees to assist him in staff affirmative action at both the School of Medicine and the Medical Center. The director of SLAC has an advisory panel to assist him in the same function.

In addition, the president of the university has been advised by two special assistants during the past few years: James E. Simmons for black affairs and Salvador D. Sanchez for Chicano affairs, a position formerly held by Luis Nogales. Both offices are being reviewed to see what changes in their functions are appropriate in the future. Gwendolyn Shunatona, assistant dean of student affairs, is available for counsel on native American matters.

The Committee on the Education and Employment of Women, mentioned earlier, has served as a useful advisory group on affirmative action. Two other general agencies have been available to individuals who wish to bring questions involving affirmative action to the attention of the administration.

The ombudsman, last year Harvey Hall, is charged with protecting "the interests and rights of members of the Stanford community from injustices or abuses of discretion, from gross inefficiency, from unnecessary delay and complication in the administration of university rules and regulations, and from inconsistency, unfairness, unresponsiveness, and prejudice in the individual's experience with university activities." Although he has no decision-making authority, he has wide powers of inquiry. He refers matters to the proper person or office, assisting, when appropriate, in negotiations.

The Human Relations Commission, over the past few years, has been available to consider complaints by persons who allege that they have been subjected to discriminatory treatment on the basis of race, color, creed, sex, or national origin. Its future role is being reviewed.

Dissemination of Policy

Recipients of Information

There are three principal emphases in the university's efforts to disseminate information about affirmative action:

1. To inform officers and managers of their responsibility for making supervisory judgments consistent with the policy and to assist in carrying out that responsibility
2. To advise members of the university community about their rights and responsibilities within affirmative action
3. To describe the program to outside organizations with which the university deals, in order to enlist their aid in matters affecting employment.

The general broad commitment and the formal affirmative action policy, as they have evolved since 1968, have been disseminated frequently in the community.

The specific practical implications of that commitment and policy,
however, have not always been clearly understood. Much of 1972-73
was spent in developing and implementing the new procedures; for example, the faculty affirmative action officer's work with search committees and the explanatory sessions with managers about the guiding
administrative memoranda for staff managers.

In 1973-73 the university continued to use the methods of dissemination of policy that had been successful in the past and added others.
To the degree that institutional priorities, legal requirements, or
new techniques of implementation are evolving—rather than static—
conditions, the need for dissemination of information will persist.

Managers and Officers. The affirmative action program and policies
are aimed at managers because they are responsible for making the
policies work. This report is written primarily for the officers and
managers who plan and implement the program, and for those outside
the university who are charged with reviewing the program as a whole.
Thus it describes the overall administrative tools, institutional commitments, and procedures. But because no system is error-free,
and universities are traditionally diffuse and decentralized, Stanford's
plan for affirmative action still depends in part upon individual employees making employment procedures work for them.

Employees. It is naive to assume that single individuals will benefit
automatically because the template of affirmative action is overlaid
on the university. If an employee believes that his or her job is improperly classified, he or she should initiate a review. An individual
must apply for the posted job that takes him/her to a higher level, not
wait to be propelled into it. An office assistant who wants to advance
should seek on-the-job or other training opportunities. And employees who feel aggrieved must press their grievances within the stated
time limits if they are to achieve redress under established procedures.

It is further important to understand that affirmative action does
not guarantee total job security. Employees will be fired for cause
or unsatisfactory performance; layoffs will occur; there will be selec-
tivity among candidates for hiring; and competition, given the small
turnover and the perceived benefits of university employment, is
stiff for most jobs.

Outside Agencies. The university's News Service routinely circu-
lates stories regarding affirmative action to outside news media; and
all advertisements for staff and faculty openings in professional journals, as well as general newspaper columns, carry the line "an equal
opportunity through affirmative action employer." The faculty and
staff sections of this report include some detail on the dissemination
of employment information to outside agencies.

It may also be well to note that the university has paid some attention to informing its 100,000 alumni about its commitment to affirmative action. Stanford alumni are largely prosperous, influential citizens who hold responsible positions in private and public enterprises, and are in a position to materially assist affirmative action in the broad context of American life. Therefore, in both university-sponsored gatherings and in those held under the auspices of the Stanford Alumni Association, faculty members and university officers have addressed alumni and parent gatherings on the subject of minorities and women. A monthly publication, The Stanford Observer, which reaches all alumni and parents, regularly carries information about the university's action in these areas.

Methods of Dissemination

Written. Last year's affirmative action plan (submitted to HEW on July 31, 1972) was distributed to the entire circulation list of Campus Report in November. The university distributed 12,400 copies to students, faculty, and staff; copies have been provided for new employees. The same procedure will be followed with the 1973 plan.

There have been a number of stories about affirmative action in the Campus Report (a biweekly publication for faculty and staff), in the Stanford Daily (the independent campus newspaper), and for the use of the outside media, distributed as news releases by the Stanford News Service.

Individual Contact. Over the past few years most of the officers, managers, deans, and department heads have dealt individually and informally with specialists of the personnel and employee relations staff and with staff legal counsel to discuss recruiting efforts and individual hiring decisions. The faculty affirmative action officer has met with members of search committees to assist them in their recruiting and, in schools in which such groups exist, with the deans' executive committees to discuss faculty affirmative action in general. Deans of the schools have met with department chairmen to discuss goals. Staff affirmative action coordinators have discussed procedures and questions with managers.

Group Sessions. Affirmative action group coordinators and unit coordinators have met to consider aspects of Stanford policy and the law, work-force priorities, and procedures of planning. Occasionally these informal procedures have been augmented by formal, didactic sessions about affirmative action, to which managers and officers are invited. On such occasions, specialists in employment can reaffirm Stanford's legal responsibility for affirmative action as well as the educational context that asserts its importance. The meetings involve the managers personally and assist them in understanding institutional goals, as well as providing a forum in which to receive their critiques of the program. In such a setting, managers can be reminded that their personal, individual responsibility for affirmative action is overlaid by a larger institutional requirement: that Stanford is responsible for their employment and faculty selection decisions.

Faculty Affirmative Action

Responsibility for Implementation

The president of the university has ultimate responsibility for the implementation of all affirmative action. He has delegated the responsibility for faculty affirmative action to the vice-president and provost, who in turn has delegated portions of that responsibility to the vice-provost for faculty affairs, Professor Arthur Bienenstock.

Professor Bienenstock also functions as the faculty affirmative action officer. His duties center on assistance to the deans in developing and implementing faculty affirmative action procedures and coordination of their efforts in the following ways:

1. To develop policies and procedures for appropriately increasing female and ethnic minority representation on the faculty and to insure that the policy is implemented

2. To review all faculty appointments and promotions, in order to determine whether they are consistent with that policy and the associated procedural guidelines

3. To aid search committees in their efforts to broaden the scope of their searches

4. To design and implement internal audit and reporting systems to measure the effectiveness of the program

5. To publish equal opportunity policies and procedural guidelines related to faculty hiring and to report on progress in faculty affirmative action

6. To administer the faculty affirmative action fund

7. An additional, informal responsibility has devolved upon the office—that of counseling young faculty members who are women or members of minority groups about professional matters. The period in which they work toward tenure is particularly difficult in terms of their own personal, professional development because of the university's heavy demands on their time for the benefit of the students.

Dissemination of Policy

During 1972-73 the faculty affirmative action officer has met individually with deans and department chairmen in order to describe
the policy and discuss the importance of realistic numerical goals.

The Faculty Senate, an elective representative group from the
Academic Council, has been the forum for numerous discussions of
faculty affirmative action objectives. In February 1973, they adopted
the following resolution:

> To implement further Stanford's commitment to wo-
> men, the Senate of the Academic Council recommends:
> That steps shall be taken that will significantly in-
> crease the number of women on the faculty;
> That as a proximal goal, the current proportionate
> representation of women among new appointees to the
> faculty be maintained; and
> That the faculty affirmative action officer shall re-
> port annually to the Senate on the representation of wo-
> men among faculty newly hired and promoted during the
> preceding year.

This statement, along with other discussions of matters affecting
women and minority faculty members, was reported to the campus
community through Campus Report and the Stanford Daily.

Implementation of Faculty Affirmative Action Policy

A number of procedural steps are taken before a faculty member
can be hired at Stanford. First, the billet must be approved, whether
it is a new position or a vacancy. Then a search committee is usually
appointed, which functions independently until it has chosen the candidates who might be offered the position. After search, a department
presents the name of the candidate of its choice for approval of the
dean, the provost, the president, and the board of trustees.

Four elements are essential if faculty affirmative action is to become a reality and if equal opportunity goals are to be met while maintaining the high quality of Stanford's appointments: extensive search,
rigorous selection, outside review of search and selection, and financial flexibility.

Faculty Search. The search for faculty members must be extensive
enough so that a search committee is likely to learn of all potential
candidates for a position. The chairman of each committee is given
clear guidelines stressing the faculty appointment policy and the university's commitment to thorough search.

Search committees are expected to inform all universities with significant activity in the field for which a vacancy exists of that vacancy, and to notify committees for minorities and for women within professional societies of the opening. They have been encouraged to advertise the opening for which they seek candidates in appropriate professional journals. And, finally, they are urged to consult women and minority-group members on campus for advice on candidates they might otherwise have missed.

Selection Process. The procedures used to select the individual to whom a position is offered must be sufficiently rigorous to insure that the best available candidate, independent of race, color, creed, religion, sex, age, or national origin, is chosen.

Review. Because each search committee functions independently until it has chosen the candidates who might be offered the position, the review process is particularly important.

In 1972 the approval form for presenting a candidate was redesigned to allow the faculty affirmative action officer and the provost's senior staff to monitor compliance of search committees. The headings of pertinent sections on the new form read as follows:

> a. List, in order of priority, candidates seriously considered for this position. For appointments to the rank of associate professor (nontenured) and for recommendations involving tenure, note after the name of each nonrecommended candidate the authors of outside letters comparing him with the recommended candidate.
>
> b. Explain the order of priority. If the recommended candidate is not the first choice, explain why higher choices are not being put forward. If the candidate is already a member of the Stanford faculty, explain why he is recommended over other individuals in the field.
>
> c. If the candidate is not a woman or a member of an ethnic minority group, indicate which of the candidates do fall within the program and describe the affirmative action search followed with respect to this appointment.

Sections (a) and (b) are designed to insure that the candidate chosen has the highest qualifications for the position and that other candidates have not been discriminated against on the basis of race, color, religion, creed, sex, age, or national origin. Section (c) is designed to insure that search committees have performed sufficiently extensive searches. If the information provided is inadequate for the assurances of appropriate search and selection procedures, the provost will not approve the appointment.

In unusual cases the provost may approve bypassing some of these procedures. These occasions occur when an outstanding individual becomes available for a faculty role that was not included within the billeted positions but that would add considerably to the university's effectiveness in carrying out its educational and research objectives. In such cases the outstanding contributions of the individual and the value of that individual's anticipated functions must be documented before the provost approves the position and the appointment.

Financial Flexibility. The faculty affirmative action fund was announced in December 1971 with an allotment of $75,000 in annually recurring—or, in Stanford nomenclature, "budget base"—money as a mechanism for taking advantage of opportunities for affirmative action. In 1973-74 the fund is set at $50,000.

The fund's general purpose is to hire individuals who are outstanding scholars and teachers, who may be expected to contribute significantly to the university's educational needs, but who may not fit exactly the specifications for an existing opening. The fund may be used in the following ways:

1. To supplement existing departmental or school budgets so that a highly desirable individual can be hired, when appropriate, at a higher rank than was anticipated when the position was defined

2. To allow departments and schools to anticipate retirement in taking advantage of available talent. The fund can finance the appointment of outstanding individuals whom departments and schools want to add to their faculties but for whom no budget position will exist until a faculty member retires—perhaps three or four years later.

3. To allow departments and schools to create new positions when special opportunities arise.

Faculty Affirmative Action—1972-73

This section describes briefly the major accomplishments of faculty affirmative action during 1972-73, aimed at the general goals of increasing the number of female and ethnic minority professorial faculty members at Stanford.

Many of the activities respond to correspondence and conversations held by the faculty affirmative action officer, the provost, and other administrative officers with the Professional Women of Stanford University Medical School, the Committee on the Education and Employment of Women, women's caucus groups from several departments, and concerned individual faculty members. They also have met with members of the Chicano faculty as a group, with individual Chicano faculty members, and with representatives of the Chicano community.

Most of these dialogues revolved about questions of fairness in the search and promotion processes. Can the university guarantee equity by procedural means? Are present procedures adequate? In other instances, these groups were asked for assistance in the identification of candidates.

Promotions and New Appointments. Since the last report, eighteen women, three blacks, two Orientals (one included also in count of women), and one native American were appointed out of a total of approximately ninety new professorial appointments. Of these, four women (including one Oriental), one native American, and one black were appointed to tenured positions.

In addition, four women currently on the faculty were promoted to tenured positions, and three women were appointed to the position of senior scientist or senior research associate, thus becoming members of the Academic Council.

Faculty Affirmative Action Fund. Approximately $50,000 of the faculty affirmative action fund was expended during the year to assist in the appointment of five faculty members. Reliance on the fund is decreasing as women and members of ethnic minority groups join the faculty through normal search procedures. Nevertheless, the fund will be maintained as a response mechanism for special opportunities.

Development of Search Procedures. The faculty affirmative action officer continued to aid in the development of search procedures in a number of ways:

1. Informing departments and schools about particular individuals.
2. Encouraging public advertising of searches at a meeting of the Academic Senate. The provost has urged all schools to consider the adoption of a policy requiring public advertising of searches. This policy has been adopted by the School of Medicine; other schools will continue to experiment with public advertising before making a policy decision.
3. Maintaining rosters of addresses of committees of minorities and women within professional societies. These were sent to many search committees.
4. In a memorandum of June 11, 1973, the provost suggested to deans and department heads that departments have a special obligation to inform their lecturers, research associates, and postdoctoral fellows of available positions.

Maternity Delay of Tenure Decisions. During 1971-72 the statement
of policy on appointment and tenure was amended by the following
clause:

> A faculty member who gives birth while serving un-
> der an appointment that accrues time toward tenure by
> length of service may, subject to any necessary reap-
> pointment, have the time after which tenure would be
> conferred by length of service extended by one year.
> No more than two such extensions shall be allowed.

During 1972-73 the provost notified deans and department heads
that the option should be exercised only as a convenience to the faculty
member involved, and should not be used by the department to delay
a decision inappropriately. The American Association of University
Professors has justifiably opposed such options because they may be
used by an institution to delay the tenure decision.

Search and Appointment Procedures. The procedure manual for the
appointment and promotion of faculty was completely rewritten to take
into account affirmative action obligations. The new procedures give
detailed guidance to search committees and departments. The manual
will be generally available when it has received final approval.

Part-Time Tenure. As noted in the 1972 affirmative action plan, the
provost in September 1971 reaffirmed existing university policy:
"There is no University-wide policy that prohibits the appointment of
regular faculty members—tenured or nontenured—at any rank on a
part-time basis." During 1972-73 one woman was appointed to the
tenured rank of professor on a part-time basis.

Appointment of Close Relatives. In the spring of 1971 the provost
clarified university policy on the appointment of close relatives to the
faculty as follows:

> It is the policy of Stanford University to seek for its
> faculty the best possible teachers and scholars, who are
> judged to be so in national (or international) search pre-
> ceding each appointment and promotion. There are no
> bars to the appointment of close relatives to the faculty
> in the same or different department, so long as each
> meets this standard.
> No faculty member, department chairman, dean, or
> other administrative officer shall vote, make recommen-
> dations, or in any way participate in the decision of any

matter that may directly affect the appointment, tenure, promotion, salary, or other status or interest of a close relative.

The policy is repeated here to further remind or to inform new faculty members of its existence.

Short-Term Appointments. The Faculty Committee on the Professoriate, which has been reviewing the entire faculty structure since 1972, has studied the short-term appointment procedures as part of its charge. In anticipation of that review, no significant changes have been made in the structure. Nevertheless, the faculty affirmative action officer has given detailed consideration to the matter of affirmative action searches for short term appointees, and the vice-provost for research has similarly considered the appointment procedures for nonfaculty research workers.

In both situations the goal was to employ search procedures consistent, with the level of appointment, for appointments that might be expected to last one year or more. At the same time it is desirable to maintain flexibility for occasions in which appointments must be made rapidly: for example, to gain a lecturer for extra sections of one or more courses in which enrollment has exceeded expectation.

A short-term appointment form has been adopted that will be circulated generally early in the autumn quarter of 1973, as have new search procedures for short-term appointments. It will take some time for all appointments of this nature to be covered by the new search procedures, because some present teaching appointees have been identified through previous search procedures.

Priorities for 1973-74

1. The Faculty Committee on the Professoriate, which has been reviewing faculty structure since 1972, will report its recommendations to the Academic Council during the forthcoming academic year. The charge to that committee follows:

> The ad hoc Senate Committee on the Professoriate at Stanford, subject to the charter and rules of the Senate, and in consultation with the provost and with the deans of the several schools, shall investigate and formulate recommendations concerning:
> a. The general procedures and policies governing appointments, reappointments, promotions, and non-reappointments of faculty members, including senior lecturers, senior research associates, and senior

scientists at Stanford University, and also the means
by which both the candidate for such appointment or
promotion and the various reviewing bodies shall be
assured of mutual understanding concerning these
procedures and policies.

b. The qualifications and prerogatives to be associated
with certain nonprofessorial academic positions
within the University, including particularly lecturers, research associates, and research scientists.

c. The qualifications and prerogatives to be associated
with professorial positions in "clinical" subjects in
the School of Medicine.

d. The means, if any, by which options for retirement
or part-time retirement at ages other than sixty-five
may be offered to the Stanford faculty.

The results of the committee's findings undoubtedly will have implications for faculty affirmative action.

2. The faculty affirmative action officer will continue to seek
methods by which to improve search and selection procedures.

3. We note that no Chicano faculty were appointed this year.
This might be anticipated from the very small number of Chicano
Ph.D. degree holders. Nevertheless, the vice-provost for faculty
affairs next year will work directly with the Chicano faculty to improve the procedures for learning about prospective Chicano faculty
members and to guarantee that appropriate department chairmen and
deans are informed about such individuals.

4. During 1971-72, the Medical School reviewed the qualifications and functions of a number of men and women whose title was
research associate. Some of these individuals were appointed to the
professorial faculty.

The position of research associate at Stanford University, however (as at similar institutions), is fraught with affirmative action
implications of a subtle, nonstatistical nature. For some individuals
it is a stepping-stone for a professorial position here or elsewhere.
For others it is a relatively permanent job in which there is little
chance of promotion. Since there are a significant number of the
latter type of jobs, the extensive representation of women in this category at Stanford University cannot be viewed as a success of affirmative action.

The nature of many of these positions can be defined when they
are created. For this reason, the next faculty affirmative action
efforts are aimed at a subdivision of this rank into a number of job
classifications. These classifications would allow for promotion and
also would indicate which positions are more of a technical aide and
associate than of an upwardly mobile nature.

11

The post-Sputnik expansion of American colleges and universities coincided with the civil rights movement of the 1960s to provide a climate conducive to the emergence of feminism on campus. The extension of civil rights legislation to include sex as well as race, and the subsequent admission of women to formerly all-male colleges, served to focus attention on the virtual absence of women from the senior ranks of faculty and administrators in institutions of higher education. This awareness developed while the academic job market was expanding, and while funds for graduate fellowships were readily available.

Government legislation outlawing discrimination, accompanied by threats of financial sanctions and the gradual change in the attitude toward working and professional women, helped to sensitize the academic community to the disparity in its ranks between men and women. A significant increase in the number of women among students at selective colleges and among nontenured faculty has occurred during the last five years. A corresponding change has not taken place among tenured faculty or at the administrative level. The obstacles in the way of progress and ways to overcome them are discussed throughout this book. There is remarkable unanimity among the contributors concerning appropriate remedial strategies.

As the academic job market has tightened and educational funding has become scarce, a growing backlash against affirmative action has begun to develop, best characterized by the recent publication of Richard Lester's Antibias Regulations of Universities. Critics of federal regulations claim to believe in affirmative action, but either cannot or will not accept the fact that women and men have equal potential as scholars and teachers. They equate affirmative action with a lowering of faculty quality. Underlying this belief is the stubborn though unsubstantiated assertion that university appointments are based exclusively on merit, and the implicit conclusion that if more women and minority group members have not been appointed, the reason must be that they lack the required merit. Ethnic origin, sex, and race, it is alleged, have never been factors that have influenced university hiring. Evidence to the contrary is overwhelming.

Affirmative action requirements have not been welcomed by academic institutions; and the commitment to the recruitment of women is grudging rather than enthusiastic. Attempts to ascribe women's underrepresentation on our faculties to their homemaking responsibilities, their lack of scholarly interest, or their preference for introductory teaching undoubtedly will continue to be made as the competition for scarce academic jobs increases. It is unlikely, however, that the younger generation of women students and faculty will accept anything less than full equality of opportunity as active scholars and participants in all phases of academic life.

Government legislation alone will not prove adequate to achieve nondiscrimination. Unless those groups affected by continued discrimination work actively and consistently to force implementation of existing legislation, to expose institutional noncompliance, and to lobby for more effective legislation where it is needed, the momentum gained during the last few years will be lost. Tradition is firmly entrenched. Resistance to change is formidable. The only hope for greater equality lies in sustained, coordinated efforts by women to gain admission to graduate and professional schools and in their determination to insist on their right to utilize their training on an equal footing with male peers. This book was written to assist and guide men and women committed to this struggle for equal opportunity.

Astin, Helen. The Woman Doctorate in America. New York: Russell Sage Foundation, 1969.

Bayer, Alan E. College and University Faculty: A Statistical Description. American Council on Education, Research Reports 5, no. 5 (1970).

Bernard, Jesse. Academic Women. University Park: Pennsylvania State University Press, 1964.

Furniss, W. Todd, and Patricia Albjerg Graham. Women in Higher Education. Washington, D.C.: American Council on Education, 1974.

Getman, Julius. "The Emerging Constitutional Principle of Sexual Equality." Supreme Court Review, 1972, p. 157.

Harris, Ann S. "The Second Sex in Academe." AAUP Bulletin 56 (September 1970): 283-95.

House of Representatives, Special Subcommittee on Education of the Committee on Education and Labor. Discrimination Against Women. Two volumes. Washington, D.C.: U.S. Government Printing Office, June 1970.

Lester, Richard. Antibias Regulations of Universities. New York: McGraw-Hill, 1974.

National Academy of Sciences. Doctorate Production in United States Universities, 1920-62. National Research Council Publication 1142. Washington, D.C.: The Academy, 1963.

New York City Commission on Human Rights. Women's Role in Contemporary Society. New York: Avon, 1972.

Oltman, Ruth M. Status of Women on Campus—Students, Administrators, Faculty, A Preliminary Research Report. Washington, D.C.: American Association of University Women, 1970.

Robinson, Lora. "The Status of Academic Women." Washington, D.C.: ERIC Clearinghouse on Higher Education, 1971.

Rossi, Alice S., and Ann Calderwood. Academic Women on the Move. New York: Russell Sage Foundation, 1973.

Sandler, Bernice. "Backlash in Academia: A Critique of the Lester Report on Affirmative Action." Teacher's College Record, February 1975.

Scully, Malcolm G. "Women in Higher Education: Challenging the Status Quo." Chronicle of Higher Education 4 (February 9, 1970): 2-5.

"Title VII and Employment Discrimination in 'Upper Level' Jobs." Columbia Law Review 73 (1973): 1614.

U.S. Department of Health, Education and Welfare. Digest of Educational Statistics—1971. Washington, D.C.: U.S. Government Printing Office, 1972.

Reports on the status of academic women at individual campuses are available through

> ERIC Clearinghouse on Higher Education
> George Washington University
> 1 Dupont Circle
> Washington, D.C. 20036

Federal laws and regulations pertaining to women in academia include the following:

Higher Education Guidelines-Executive Order 11246, available from Regional Office for Civil Rights or from Division of Higher Education, Office for Civil Rights, Department of HEW, Washington, D.C. 20201. This publication includes the provisions of Revised Order no. 4, sex discrimination guidelines, Titles VI and VII of the Civil Rights Act of 1964, and Title IX of the Education Amendments of 1972.

"Proposed Rules of the Department of Health, Education and Welfare for Implementation of Title IX of the Education Amendments of 1972," Federal Register 39 (June 20, 1974): 22228. These rules are not final. Comments were due at HEW by October 15, 1974. Final rules will be published sometime in 1975.

Equal Employment Opportunity Commission, 25-26, 80
equal opportunities, goals for (long-range), 83-85; goals for (short-range), 85-92; solutions to problems of, 126-127, 136-138
Equal Pay Act of 1963, 20, 26-27, 63, 80
Equal Protection Clause, 5
Executive Order 11246, 21-23, 37, 38
Executive Order 11375, 21-23, 46, 140, 149

flexibility in academic rules and schedules, effect on women, 117-119
fringe benefits, specific programs for equity in, 65-66
future programs for affirmative action, 53

goals, techniques and timetables for, 50-51
goals versus quotas, 11-17; 22, 30-32, 37-41

HEW (see, Department of Health, Education and Welfare)
Higher Education Guidelines, 46
Hornig, Lilli S., 8-19

intellectual ability, sex differences in, 107-114

legal aspects of discrimination, 20-36, 46-53
litigation, outlook for, 32-33

Miner, Anne S., 139-162

nepotism, 61-62

Nurse Training Amendments Act, 27

OFCC (see, Office of Federal Contract Compliance)
Office for Civil Rights, 37, 41, 46, 79
Office of Federal Contract Compliance, 21, 28, 46-53, 68-69, 73
ombudsman, observations of relative to universities, 120-127

Pottinger, J. Stanley, 37-44
promotions, specific programs for equity in, 63-64
Public Health Service Act, 20

quotas versus goals, 11-17, 22, 30-32, 37-41

rank, specific programs for equity in, 63-64
records, requirements for in affirmative action programs, 133
recruitment, of science students, 116-117; specific programs for, 55-58
reverse discrimination, 25, 41-42

salaries, data on, 134; equality of for women, 92-107; specific programs for equity in, 62-63
Sandler, Bernice, 20-36
science, opportunities for women in, 115-119
Scott, Elizabeth L., 82-114
selection processes, specific programs for equity in, 58-62

168

ARIE Y. LEWIN is Associate Professor of Management and Behavioral Science and director of the Social Policy and Urban Affairs Program at the Graduate School of Business Administration, New York University. He is the author of Behavioral Aspects of Accounting (Prentice-Hall) and Policy Sciences: Methodology and Cases (Pergamon). Dr. Lewin received a B.S. in engineering and an M.S. in operations research from the University of California at Los Angeles, and his Ph.D. in industrial administration from Carnegie-Mellon University.

ELGA WASSERMAN is currently a second-year student at the Yale Law School. Previously she served as Special Assistant to the President of Yale University on the Education of Women, and as Assistant Dean of the Yale Graduate School. She is co-author with Ellen Switzer of the Random House Guide to Graduate Study. Dr. Wasserman received her B.A. degree summa cum laude from Smith College, and a Ph.D. in chemistry from Harvard University.

LINDA H. BLEIWEIS is on the staff of the Vice-Chancellor for Faculty and Staff Relations of the City University of New York. She previously served as Administrator of the Department of Social Service of the Albert Einstein College of Medicine-Bronx Municipal Hospital Center. Ms. Bleiweis holds a B.A. from Queen's College of the City of New York and an M.B.A. from New York University Graduate School of Business Administration.

RUTH I. BEACH is affirmative action officer at Carnegie-Mellon University. Previously Dr. Beach was a psychotherapist and sex counselor at Princeton University. She received her bachelor's degree in psychology from Antioch College and earned her Ph.D. in clinical psychology from Columbia University.

MARY I. BUNTING is presently at Princeton University as Assistant to the President for Special Projects. Before coming to Princeton, she was President of Radcliffe College. She has taught at Bennington College, Goucher College, Wellesley College, Harvard, and Yale, and served as Dean of Douglass College. Dr. Bunting was a member of the Atomic Energy Commission and President Kennedy's Commission on the Status of Women. She received her B.A. in physics from Vassar College and her M.A. and Ph.D. in agricultural bacteriology and chemistry from the University of Wisconsin.

ALICE H. COOK is currently preparing a series of monographs on the conditions and problems of working mothers in nine countries, a study sponsored by the Ford Foundation. She is professor emerita at Cornell University where she was a member of the faculty of the School of Industrial and Labor Relations. She is the author of Japanese Trade Unionism and of numerous articles on labor relations. Dr. Cook did her undergraduate work at Northwestern University and her graduate work in Germany.

LILLI S. HORNIG is Executive Director of Higher Education Resource Services, a project cosponsored by the Ford Foundation and Brown University to improve the opportunities and status of women in faculty and administrative posts. She has taught chemistry at Radcliffe and Brown, and chaired the chemistry department at Trinity College, Washington, D.C. Dr. Hornig received her A.B. from Bryn Mawr College and her M.A. and Ph.D. in chemistry from Harvard.

ANNE S. MINER has served as Stanford's Affirmative Action Officer since 1972. Prior to her professional involvement with the issue of women in higher education, Ms. Miner was Associate Director of the Stanford Annual Fund. She has also served as Research Assistant at the Mental Research Institute in Palo Alto. Ms. Miner is a graduate of Radcliffe College.

STANLEY POTTINGER is assistant attorney general, Civil Rights Division, Justice Department of the United States. He was previously director of the Office of Civil Rights, and assistant to the Secretary of Civil Rights at HEW. He has had articles published in the California Law Review, Journal of the American Institute of Planners, Integrated Education, The Harvard Center for Law and Education and Change magazine.

BERNICE SANDLER is Director of the Project on the Status and Education of Women, Association of American Colleges. She previously served as Deputy Director of the Women's Action Program at HEW, as Education Specialist for the U.S. House of Representatives' Special Subcommittee on Education, and as chairperson of the Action Committee for Federal Contract Compliance of the Women's Equity Action League. Dr. Sandler holds a degree in counseling and personnel services from the University of Maryland.

ELIZABETH L. SCOTT is Professor of Statistics at the University of California, Berkeley. She is a member of the Committee on National Statistics of the National Academy of Sciences. Dr. Scott is the author or more than 90 professional articles as well as coeditor of several books. She received her B.A. and Ph.D. from the University of California, Berkeley in astronomy.

LENORE J. WEITZMAN is Assistant Professor of Sociology at the University of California, Davis. She has written extensively on the legal status of women and on sex role socialization. Dr. Weitzman received her Ph.D. from Columbia University and completed postdoctoral work at the Yale Law School as a Russell Sage Fellow.

MALE AND FEMALE GRADUATE STUDENTS: The
Question of Equal Opportunity

Lewis C. Solmon

TRADE UNION WOMEN: A Study of their Participation in
New York City Locals

Barbara M. Wertheimer
Anne H. Nelson

WOMEN'S INFERIOR EDUCATION: An Economic Analysis
Blanche Fitzpatrick

THE WORLD'S STUDENTS IN THE UNITED STATES:
A Review and Evaluation of Research on Foreign Students
Seth Spaulding
Michael Flack